The Gospel in Action

ALLAN K. BURGESS & MAX H. MOLGARD

BOOKCRAFT
Salt Lake City, Utah

Library of Congress Catalog Card Number: 92-71845
ISBN 0-88494-836-6

First Printing, 1992

Printed in the United States of America

Contents

Introduction vii

1 Go to the Football Field 1

2 Thy Will Be Done 5

3 A Miraculous Birth 10

4 A Nonmember Dad 15

5 A Promise Comes True 19

6 To Every Thing There Is a Season 25

7 Russian People Respond to the Gospel 29

8 Don't Worry About Him 36

9 It Was Broken 40

10 Visit Sister Smith.. 45

11 A Heavenly Choir 48

12 Don't Worry—It's Me 53

13 Please Ask Them to Come Again 57

14 Peanuts 61

15 Yielding Her Heart unto God................................ 66

16 He Needed Long-Sleeved Cotton Shirts...................... 70

17 Let's Say a Little Prayer................................... 76

18 Standing Up for the Right.................................. 80

19 The Very Night 84

20 Hope Replaced Despair..................................... 90

21 The Gift of Tongues.. 95

22 I Gave Them the Sleeping Bag 99

23 Carlos.. 104

24 The Surprise Call.. 108

25 Jesus Does! 112

26 Miguel Had No Shoes....................................... 117

27 From Trials to Blessings.................................... 121

28 A Glimpse Beyond the Veil 126

29 The Message Had Been Delivered 130

Introduction

The stories of faith, love, courage, and dedication contained in this book can strengthen our testimonies and inspire us to live better lives. They cover a wide range of topics that can enrich home evenings, Church lessons, talks, and personal study. Only those stories that could be verified have been included.

Selected quotations from the scriptures, Church leaders, and Church writers accompany each story in order to make it an even more useful resource for both teaching and personal study. An effort has been made to closely correlate the quotations and the stories.

The authors deeply appreciate those who were willing to share with us their experiences so that others could benefit and grow. It is inspiring to read about the divine intervention that occurred in their lives.

We feel impressed to point out, however, that God does not always protect us from harm or grant every request that we might make of him. This does not necessarily mean that we are less worthy than someone else or in disfavor with God. President Spencer W. Kimball said: "Being human, we would expel from our lives physical pain and mental anguish and assure ourselves of continual ease and comfort, but if we were to close the doors upon sorrow and distress, we might be excluding our greatest friends and benefactors. Suffering can make saints of people as they learn patience, long-suffering, and self-mastery. The sufferings of our Savior were part of his education." (*Tragedy or Destiny?* [Salt Lake City: Deseret Book Co., 1977], p. 3.)

Moreover, our not receiving specifically what we ask for does not mean that God will not give us what we need. His concerns are eternal in nature while, most of the time, we are struggling with daily challenges and limited perspective.

Although many of us may experience strong spiritual events at times in our lives, the Lord usually guides and blesses us in quiet, simple ways. Elder Boyd K. Packer said that "strong, impressive spiritual experiences do not come to us very frequently. . . . We become taller in testimony like we grow taller in physical stature; we hardly know it happens because it comes by growth." ("The Candle of the Lord," *Ensign*, January 1983, p. 53.)

1

And I was led by the Spirit,
not knowing beforehand
the things which I should do.
—1 Nephi 4:6

Go to the
Football Field

When Ken was twelve or thirteen years old, he once accompanied his father to the local trash dump. His dad was driving their truck, and Ken was sitting on the passenger side, near the door. As he was looking out of the window, he had a feeling that he should move away from the door and sit next to his father. He ignored the feeling; but it came again so strongly that he immediately slid away from the door. A few moments later, when his father made a turn, the door that Ken had been leaning against flew open. He didn't think much about it at the time; but later, when he came to recognize how the Spirit operates, he realized that he had been saved from serious injury or death by his Father in Heaven.

Ken had another spiritual experience when he was sixteen. His family had moved from Tooele to the small town of Grantsville, about fifteen miles away. However, Ken kept his job at a clothing store in downtown Tooele. Early one summer morning, as he approached the outskirts of Tooele, he had a feeling that he should drive over by the high school. The high school was not on his way to work, and he had no idea why he should go there; but he decided to respond to this feeling, and he drove toward the school. As he drove slowly by the front of the school, he didn't see or hear anything out of the ordinary. He felt a little puzzled, but decided to turn left toward town, since it was time for him to get to work.

Before Ken could turn, however, he received a stronger impression that he should turn right, not left, and that he should go behind the school. He followed the direction, but still didn't see or hear anything that would cause any concern. As he went to pull out from behind the school, Ken heard an actual voice telling him to drive to the far end of the parking lot, next to the football field.

The football field was located on top of a hill. Steps led up to the playing field and to the bleachers. Behind the bleachers the hill sloped down, and the field was surrounded by a chain-link fence. Ken drove past the football field, to the end of the parking lot, and started his return trip. As he rounded the corner of the parking lot, still seeing nothing of any consequence, he saw a body lying by the chain-link fence.

Ken now knew why he was there, but the sight of the body really frightened him. He had no idea who it was. He jumped out of his car and sprinted to the entrance of the football field, up the stairs, and across the field. As soon as he had dashed partway down the hill, he recognized the person lying there as his best friend. His friend's head, neck, and shoulder were covered with blood, and he was lying motionless.

When Ken saw his friend in this condition, he almost went to pieces. He thought the boy was dead. Then a calm feeling came over him, and he approached the inert body. As Ken turned him over, his friend stirred and looked up at him, and Ken realized he was still alive.

His friend was in a very dazed condition, as if he was just coming out of unconsciousness. Ken picked him up, carried him to his car, and rushed him to the hospital. He was afraid that he might die if he left him alone while he went for help.

Much later, when he had regained consciousness, the friend told Ken what had happened. He had been working with two other men, clearing weeds and debris from along the fence. The two men had left to take a load of junk to the county dump. He was left alone. As he had continued to clear the fence, he had encountered a large rock that he could not budge. He grabbed a pick and took several swings at the rock, but it stubbornly refused to move. He then took an extra large swing with the pick, but the tip struck the chain-link fence and the pick turned sideways in his hand. Instead of hitting the rock, the end of the pick hit him in the back of his head and opened a large wound. The doctor said that the wound was severe enough that, if Ken had not come along, his friend might have bled to death before his fellow workers returned.

The gravity of his friend's situation did not hit Ken until later. He then came to appreciate how the Lord had worked through him, a young Aaronic Priesthood holder, in saving his friend from possible death. He began to better understand the promptings of the Spirit and to cherish the spiritual experiences of his youth.

Inspiration

We Can Receive Pure Intelligence

"The Lord has a way of pouring pure intelligence into our minds to prompt us, to guide us, to teach us, to warn us. You can know the things you need to know *instantly!* Learn to receive inspiration." (Boyd K. Packer, "Prayers and Answers," *Ensign*, November 1979, p. 20.)

Personal Radio Tubes

" . . . You and I have within our souls something like what might be said to be a counterpart of . . . radio tubes. We might have what we call a 'go-to-sacrament-meeting' tube, a 'keep-the-Word-of-Wisdom' tube, a 'pay-your-tithing' tube, a 'have-your-family-prayers' tube, a 'read-the-scriptures' tube, and, as one of the most important—one that might be said to be the master tube of our whole soul—we have what we might call the 'keep-yourselves-morally-clean' tube. If one of these becomes worn out by disuse or inactivity—if we fail to keep the commandments of God—it has the same effect upon our spiritual selves that a worn-out tube has in a radio." (Harold B. Lee, *Stand Ye in Holy Places* [Salt Lake City: Deseret Book Co., 1974], p. 137.)

The Importance of Trusting in the Spirit

"And I was led by the Spirit, not knowing beforehand the things which I should do" (1 Nephi 4:6).

How Does Revelation Usually Come?

"Yea, behold, I will tell you in your mind and in your heart, by the Holy Ghost, which shall come upon you and which shall dwell in your heart.

"Now, behold, this is the spirit of revelation." (D&C 8:2-3.)

2

*Trust in the Lord with all thine heart; and
lean not unto thine own understanding.
In all thy ways acknowledge him, and he
shall direct thy paths.*
—Proverbs 3:5-6

Thy Will
Be Done

Art taught seminary five days a week, yet he had much to learn about Heavenly Father and about how he works.

Art and his wife, Jan, had been looking forward to a three-day workshop at Brigham Young University. These workshops for seminary teachers were held each summer, and they had become a highlight of each year for Art and Jan. They both enjoyed the opportunity to learn more about the gospel, and it gave them a chance to get away from the children and to be together as a couple.

The day before they were scheduled to leave for the workshop, one of their sons, Brian, developed a high fever. He did not feel sick, but Art and Jan felt that they could not leave him until his fever was gone. They did everything they could to help him, but his temperature increased.

Soon it was the night before they were to leave, and the chances of going to the workshop were getting slimmer by the minute. They had prayed many times during the last twenty-four hours that God would help their son get better, but there had been no improvement. As the night wore on, Art became increasingly irritated. His prayers became more demanding in nature, as he proceeded to tell God what was best for Art and for his family.

At nine o'clock they put Brian to bed with his fever. Every hour they woke him up long enough to take his temperature. It remained the same. But at each bed check, Art's blood pressure seemed to rise a little higher.

Finally, about midnight, after another unsuccessful check on Brian, Art went into his bedroom and got after Heavenly Father. He told him how he and Jan had been looking forward to the workshop for many months. He reminded him that they were going there so he could be a better teacher and so they could become better parents. He asked him why he promised that he would answer prayers, but refused to answer theirs.

Following this tirade, Art sat on his bed and thought about what he had just done. He thought back on the prayers that he had offered over the course of the past two days. He realized that he had not been requesting; he had been demanding. He had been so sure that going to the workshop was the right thing to do that he had failed to ask God what he thought about it. He had approached God as he would approach a smor- gasbord—considering only his own desires and expecting to take away only what he wanted.

As Art sat pondering the arrogance he had shown, the Holy Ghost came into his heart and worked on him until he was truly humbled. Art then got on his knees and begged God to forgive his previous attitude and actions. He confessed to the Lord that he did not really know what was best. He told God that if, for some reason, he did not want Jan and him to go to the workshop, it was okay with him. He followed the example of Jesus in the Garden of Gethsemane; he said, "Thy will be done," and he really meant it.

As he ended his prayer, he felt a feeling of calm and peace enter his heart. He sat down with Jan and told her what had taken place. It had only been a few minutes since they had checked on Brian, but now they both felt they should go check on him again. The Lord had interceded in their behalf, and Brian's fever was gone.

Art returned to his bedroom and thanked God for his great goodness and mercy. This time tears filled his eyes as, once again, he asked the Lord to forgive him.

The three-day workshop was a tremendous help to both Art and Jan. But Art learned a lot more during the two days preceding the workshop than he did in any of the classes. He learned to trust God and to accept his will, even though it may not coincide with his personal desires. He learned that, when our hearts are wrong, we restrict the blessings that we can receive, because God cannot bless us in our wickedness. He learned that God truly does love us and will do everything he can to help us become more like him.

Thy Will Be Done

You Can Do with Me What You Want

" . . . I want to be good. I'm not ashamed to say that—I want to be good. And I've found in my life that it has been critically important that this was established between me and the Lord so that I knew that He knew which way I had committed my agency. I went before Him in essence and said, 'I'm not neutral, and You can do with me what You want. If You need my vote, it's there. I don't care what You do with me, and You don't have to take anything from me because I give it to You— everything, all I own, all I am.' And that makes the difference." (Boyd K. Packer, *"That All May Be Edified"* [Salt Lake City: Bookcraft, 1982], p. 272.)

God Can Do More with Us Than We Can

" . . . Men and women who turn their lives over to God will find out that he can make a lot more out of their lives than they can. He will deepen their joys, expand their vision, quicken their minds, strengthen their muscles, lift their spirits, multiply their blessings, increase their opportunities, comfort their souls, raise up friends, and pour out peace. Whoever will lose his life to God will find he has eternal life." (Ezra Taft

Benson, "Jesus Christ—Gifts and Expectations," *New Era*, May 1975, p. 20.)

Delight to Do God's Will

"I delight to do thy will, O my God: yea, thy law is within my heart" (Psalm 40:8).

Jesus Followed the Will of the Father

"Yea, even so he shall be led, crucified, and slain, the flesh becoming subject even unto death, the will of the Son being swallowed up in the will of the Father" (Mosiah 15:7).

Trust in God

Trust the Lord—He Knows What He Is Doing

"In many ways, the world is like a jungle, with dangers that can harm or mutilate your body, enslave or destroy your mind, or decimate your morality. It was intended that life be a challenge, not so that you would fail, but that you might succeed through overcoming. You face on every hand difficult but vitally important decisions. There is an array of temptations, destructive influences, and camouflaged dangers, the like of which no previous generation has faced. I am persuaded that today no one, no matter how gifted, strong, or intelligent, will avoid serious problems without seeking the help of the Lord. . . .

"Trust in the Lord. He knows what He is doing. He already knows of your problems. And He is waiting for you to ask for help." (Richard G. Scott, "Trust in the Lord," *Ensign*, May 1989, p. 36.)

Trust with All Thine Heart

"Trust in the Lord with all thine heart; and lean not unto thine own understanding.

"In all thy ways acknowledge him, and he shall direct thy paths." (Proverbs 3:5-6.)

Learning Is Good, If We Hearken to God

"O that cunning plan of the evil one! O the vainness, and the frailties, and the foolishness of men! When they are learned they think they are wise, and they hearken not unto the counsel of God, for they set it aside, supposing they know of themselves, wherefore, their wisdom is foolishness and it profiteth them not. And they shall perish.

"But to be learned is good if they hearken unto the counsels of God." (2 Nephi 9:28-29.)

3

*And now, O all ye that have imagined up unto
yourselves a god who can do no miracles, I
would ask of you, have all these things passed,
of which I have spoken? . . . I say unto you, Nay;
and God has not ceased to be a God of miracles.*
—Mormon 9:15

A Miraculous
Birth

While working in Labor and Delivery at a large hospital, Kori had an experience that she will never forget. A woman who was in labor with her fifth pregnancy was brought to her unit. Kori learned that the woman's doctor had told her to never get pregnant again after her fourth child. Her uterus had been completely damaged during childbirth, and her last two children had been delivered by Caesarean section. Because she had not followed her regular doctor's advice, he had refused to treat her.

She arrived at the hospital in a desperate condition and in need of immediate care. The doctor on call had heard about her case and had initially refused to deliver her, but, under pressure from several of the nurses, he relented.

Kori immediately introduced herself to the expectant mother and connected a fetal monitor. While this was taking place, the woman told Kori that she had been promised in a priesthood blessing that she would deliver a normal, healthy child, and that all would be well. This woman had joined the Church one month after she had become pregnant, and even though her former physician had counseled her to get an abortion, she had refused. Her faith was unwavering concerning her child and her priesthood blessing.

As Kori connected the fetal monitor, she noticed there was no sign of movement or of a fetal heartbeat. She quickly called the on-call physician, and he ordered an ultrasound examination of the baby to determine if there was any life. The exam indicated no signs of life.

This didn't seem to have any effect on the mother. She said she had seen her baby girl in a dream and she knew that she would be born alive and well. About this time her husband arrived in the labor room, and Kori explained to him that the baby was dead. She told him that the doctor would be doing a Caesarean section to assist delivery, as the uterus was incapable of contracting.

The husband left, then quickly returned with two missionaries who lived in a trailer home next to the hospital. The missionaries gave her a blessing and promised her she would deliver a normal, healthy baby.

Kori finished preparing the mother for surgery, then wheeled her into the delivery suite. Kori took the doctor aside and told him that the mother had seen a dream depicting her child as normal and healthy. She also told him that the mother had received two priesthood blessings and that both of them had promised her that her child would live.

The doctor scoffed, enjoyed a robust laugh, and asked Kori what she really expected. Kori answered that miracles happen when the Lord makes a promise. On this note the surgery began.

After the layers of abdominal muscles were incised, the uterus was exposed. Its blackened, hardened, irregular surface denoted a very stressed and infected organ. As the doctor cut into the uterus, no blood was seen coming forth as would normally happen. Soon the bag of waters was ruptured, and an initially lifeless female child was born.

Within seconds the baby was handed to Kori. After a quick assessment, she placed the suction catheter down the baby's tiny mouth and brought forth 20 cc of clear mucous. As the tip of the catheter was pulled out of her mouth, the baby opened her eyes and looked into Kori's. Her little fingers moved, and she began to breathe. Kori immediately gave her some oxygen and dried her. It took about five minutes for the new arrival to get some color into her body, but she was very much alive.

Meanwhile the doctor was focusing on the placenta and umbilical cord. He called Kori over and said, "Look. There aren't three drops of blood here. The cord is gone and the placenta is hard!" When Kori looked at him, she noticed that he had tears in his eyes, and he said, "I want to know more about your church!"

In one month the skeptical doctor was baptized into The Church of Jesus Christ of Latter-day Saints. The birth had been a powerful witness to both the doctor and Kori that the gospel of Jesus Christ is here on the earth today and that God's power is manifest through the priesthood.

Miracles

We Should Have Faith in Miracles

"I add my personal witness that prayer, including priesthood prayer, is the proof of our faith. And the proof is rewarded by the Holy Ghost (and holy power) which Nephi said, 'will show unto you *all* things that ye should do' (2 Nephi 32:5). There are miracles of faith, and we should have faith in the miraculous.

"When Jesus called Peter to come to Him across the water, Peter, for one brief, glorious moment, forgot he did not know how and strode with ease across the sea. This is how we are meant to be." (Patricia T. Holland, "Walking on the Water," *Brigham Young University 1983-84 Fireside and Devotional Speeches* [Provo, Utah: University Publications, 1984], p. 52.)

God Still Performs Marvelous Miracles Today

"And now, O all ye that have imagined up unto yourselves a god who can do no miracles, I would ask of you, have all these things passed, of which I have spoken? Has the end come yet? Behold I say unto you, Nay; and God has not ceased to be a God of miracles.

"Behold, are not the things that God hath wrought marvelous in our eyes? Yea, and who can comprehend the marvelous works of God?" (Mormon 9:15-16.)

Miracles Are Wrought by Faith

" . . . For it is by faith that miracles are wrought; and it is by faith that angels appear and minister unto men; wherefore, if these things have ceased wo be unto the children of men, for it is because of unbelief, and all is vain" (Moroni 7:37).

Priesthood Blessings

Healings Follow True Believers

"Healings come because of faith. They are gifts of the Spirit, some persons having 'faith to be healed,' others being endowed with 'faith to heal.' Healings are among the signs that follow true believers, and the faithful elders have power to perform healings whenever it is required of them by those who have faith to be healed. As with other signs and miracles, if there are no healings among church members, such people are not the saints of God." (Bruce R. McConkie, *Mormon Doctrine*, 2d ed. [Salt Lake City: Bookcraft, 1966], p. 345.)

All Manner of Healings Are Promised to the Faithful

"And whoso shall ask it in my name in faith, they shall cast out devils; they shall heal the sick; they shall cause the blind to receive their sight, and the deaf to hear, and the dumb to speak, and the lame to walk" (D&C 35:9).

God's Will Is an Important Ingredient in Priesthood Blessings

"And the elders of the church, two or more, shall be called, and shall pray for and lay their hands upon them in my name; and if they die they shall die unto me, and if they live they shall live unto me. . . .

"And again, it shall come to pass that he that hath faith in me to be healed, and is not appointed unto death, shall be healed." (D&C 42:44, 48.)

4

A Nonmember Dad

Bette grew up in a home with two loving parents. She had a brother and two sisters. They were taught that they should pray before they went to bed and at every meal. They went on a summer vacation every year as a family. They had camped on their way to Mexico, across the country to Washington, D.C., and up the West Coast. They fished together and went on Sunday drives. They had family traditions for Christmas and birthdays. They attended church every Sunday, even when they were on vacation. The parents had high standards for their children, and the children were good students and good citizens in their community.

Bette's brother went on a mission to Sweden, and her parents went to Sweden to bring him home after a successful mission.

Drugs and alcohol were not used in their home. No one abused the children; in fact, quite the opposite. Both parents went to every activity that was important to the children. They went to hundreds of swimming meets and piano recitals, and they listened to each talk and special musical number given in church. Both of Bette's parents were there to watch when each child was blessed, baptized, and confirmed.

But *watch* was a key word. Bette's dad, Ken, would always watch the ordinances, but he couldn't participate in them because he was not a member of the Church. He was an Episcopalian.

Somehow, for some people, the fact that their family was a part-member family cancelled many of the good things they could see in the family. It was as if most of the Church members they came in contact with saw an imaginary Nonmember sign when they looked at Bette's dad. True, he was a nonmember. But he was so much more than that.

The family always went to midnight Christmas services and Easter services with their dad. Bette wondered if most of the Episcopalians hung Nonmember signs on them.

But something happened that changed everyone's signs.

Ken contracted a particularly fast-moving cancer that took him from healthy at Christmas, to terrific pain through the month of January, and to a hospitalization that lasted only a week.

Ken belonged to a small congregation of Episcopalians in Brigham City, Utah. He had studied for several years to become a lay deacon in his church. He received no pay, but spent many, many hours in service. In his schooling he had become close to other deacons, priests, and even to the Episcopal bishop of Utah. Many of these people came to the hospital. Some came several times, even though the hospital was many miles from where they lived. And, Bette thought, they brought such a beautiful spirit of love for her dad. Their prayers with the family were full of love, and Bette marveled at the beautiful, spiritual feeling that they brought with them.

When Bette's dad died, February 5, the people from both congregations poured into her parent's home. They all brought food and concern, and they filled the home with a love that tore down signs on both sides.

But there were still many worries. Bette's dad had wanted an Episcopal funeral service, but her mom needed consolation from her church also. It wasn't long, however, before their fears of hurting the members of either church were quickly put to rest.

It was a beautiful service, with the Episcopal church filled with Latter-day Saints and Episcopalians. Ken's grandchildren sang "I Am a Child of God," and many in the congregation shed tears together. Bette's husband (a seminary teacher) spoke as a representative of the family.

Episcopal priesthood leaders, in their robes, conducted the services. The last song was a favorite of Ken's, "Hold High the Cross." It was a beautiful song, and Bette thought she heard angels singing along during the last verse. Ken was buried in the deacon's robe that he was so proud of.

The dinner after the services was a combined effort of Relief Society ladies and Episcopalian ladies. They had coordinated the effort so that everyone could help.

After the funeral, Bette sat back and contemplated the many gifts that her dad had given her, and she knew that one of the best gifts was the gift of love for people who are not members of her church. Ken's funeral had been testimony to what the whole family had lived: We are all children of God.

Brotherhood and Fellowship

We Are All Brothers and Sisters

"We are all brothers and sisters born of the same Father in the spirit. . . .

"Do we sometimes regard human brotherhood as a pretty theory rather than as a divine fact? Have we truly learned the lesson that man to man we must act not as enemies, not just as acquaintances, not even as mere friends—but as brothers?" (Ezra Taft Benson, *The Teachings of Ezra Taft Benson* [Salt Lake City: Bookcraft, 1988], p. 272.)

Those Around Us Are Our Brothers and Sisters

"Each of us has more opportunities to do good and to be good than we ever use. These opportunities lie all around us. . . .

"We must remember that those mortals we meet in parking lots, offices, elevators, and elsewhere are that portion of mankind

God has given us to love and to serve. It will do us little good to speak of the general brotherhood of mankind if we cannot regard those who are all around us as our brothers and sisters." (Spencer W. Kimball, *The Teachings of Spencer W. Kimball*, ed. Edward L. Kimball [Salt Lake City: Bookcraft, 1982], p. 483.)

Let Us Cultivate a Spirit of Brotherhood

"We *can* reach out to help one another as neighbors and associates, extending even beyond our own brothers and sisters in the Church, to assist any in trouble or want wherever they may be. . . .

"Let us as Latter-day Saints cultivate a spirit of brotherhood in all of our associations." (Gordon B. Hinckley, "Let Us Move This Work Forward," *Ensign*, November 1985, p. 85.)

Extend a Hand of Fellowship to All

" . . . I believe we members do not have the option to extend the hand of fellowship only to relatives, close friends, certain Church members, and those selected nonmembers who express an interest in the Church. Limiting or withholding our fellowship seems to me to be contrary to the gospel of Jesus Christ. The Savior offered the effects of his atoning sacrifice to all mankind." (M. Russell Ballard, "The Hand of Fellowship," *Ensign*, November 1988, p. 28.)

5

A Promise
Comes True

The spring of 1984 found Darrell unemployed for the first time in his life. Because of health problems, he had been forced to change occupations, and since his new teaching job wouldn't begin until the fall, he and his family now faced five months without income.

They prepared for this problem, first, by selling their home. With the money from this sale, along with their savings, they paid cash for a real fixer-upper house located on a half acre of property in a rural community.

With a lot of hard work, Darrell and his wife, Hjordis, made the basement of the house barely livable, Their two children, at ages nine and six, shared one small bedroom; Darrell and Hjordis shared the other one. The floors were old, pockmarked cement, and the interior doors were hanging blankets. They bought a bathroom sink and toilet at a yard sale, and the tub was one that they had found abandoned in the backyard. It was one of those old, deep tubs that sat on four legs. With the application of a little rust remover and some enamel paint, it seemed to function quite well.

The main floor of the house had been gutted and had become the home for several hives of bees. The stairs to the main floor consisted of several rickety ammunition boxes, stacked on top of each other. Darrell installed a hot-water heater. His family was in the homemaking business again.

The front and back yards were mostly a fire hazard. Among the numerous weeds, however, there were four or five fruit trees and an old chicken coop. With a borrowed Rototiller and lots of muscle, Darrell and his family turned the entire backyard into a vegetable and fruit garden that they were very proud of. In order to get some semblance of lawn in the front, they dug up and transplanted lawn from a neighbor's yard where he was making a place to park his truck and camper.

Such were the conditions Darrell's family was living under when they were forced to turn to Heavenly Father and his promises from the scriptures.

Their food storage, plus judicious budgeting of their remaining savings, looked to be just enough to keep the family eating until the garden could support them. They knew that when Darrell started teaching in the fall, it would take many months to catch up financially. So a bountiful harvest from their garden was a real necessity.

The garden sprouted, and everything was looking good. They were quite proud that they were handling the most difficult challenge they had ever faced, completely on their own, without any help from anyone else. Even though they didn't have much, it felt good to know that their plan was working. And work it did—until the advent of the grasshoppers.

The year 1984 was one of those years when conditions were just right for nature to produce grasshoppers in epidemic proportions. From their backyard all the way to the mountains stretched unused fields filled with wild rye, June grass, and numerous kinds of weeds. These fields seemed a perfect habitat for these hordes of insects, with their voracious appetites. There were so many grasshoppers that if a person didn't keep his mouth closed when passing through the fields, he would end up with an unwelcome breakfast. Within every few square feet, hundreds of grasshoppers could be found.

The grasshoppers didn't cause much of a problem until the weeds in the fields dried out. It was then that the grasshoppers seemed to discover the green, succulent plants on the other side of the barbed wire. Overnight Darrell's garden turned into a cafeteria for grasshoppers.

Nothing the family did seemed to have any effect at all. Spraying worked on the grasshoppers already in the garden, but these were quickly replaced by new recruits from the other side of the fence. The family even turned their chickens into the garden. That made their chickens quite happy, but they just couldn't eat fast enough to keep up with the intruders. It seemed that their much-needed vegetables were doomed to destruction.

On a fast Sunday Darrell and his wife finally realized that turning to the Lord was the only option they had left. They were reading the familiar scripture in the third chapter of Malachi. They had read it many times before, but this time they read it with a real need, and they received enlightened understanding. They had always paid a full tithe and given fast offerings, but they had never thought much about the blessings they had received.

For the first time, verse 11 had real meaning for them: "And I will rebuke the devourer for your sakes, and he shall not destroy the fruits of your ground."

They had always felt that this promise of protection referred to the devouring fire that would take place at the Second Coming, but this time they thought about a more immediate blessing. They were facing a real devourer in their garden that truly was destroying the fruits of their ground. Darrell's family needed a fulfillment of this promise from the Lord to tithe payers, and they needed it right away. Accordingly, they knelt in prayer as a family and pleaded with the Lord to protect their garden from the devouring grasshoppers.

And God blessed them. There were still just as many grasshoppers in the fields behind their home and in other gardens in their community, but their garden was left alone. Where there had been hundreds of grasshoppers in their garden before, now there were only a few. It was as if there were an invisible, high wall around their garden which could be surmounted by only a few grasshoppers. Their harvest that year was plentiful; it fed them throughout the fall and winter and even into the next spring, when they were finally able to start catching up financially.

Darrell and his family learned many things about faith and humility. They learned that we can be blessed when we are compelled to be humble, but that when we humble ourselves, we receive even greater blessings (see Alma 32:13-15). They will be forever grateful for the harvest of understanding from that summer.

Humility

Afflictions Can Bring Humility

" . . . I rejoice in afflictions, for they are necessary to humble and prove us, that we may comprehend ourselves, become acquainted with our weakness and infirmities; and I rejoice when I triumph over them, because God answers my prayers, therefore I feel to rejoice all the day long" (John Taylor, in *Journal of Discourses* 1:17).

Our Gifts Are like Jars Covered with Macaroni

"One Christmas, my Cub Scout son needed two dollars to make me a present. On Christmas morning, he was so excited about it that in spite of the many brightly wrapped packages with his name on them, he insisted I open his present first. It was a pencil holder for my office—made from a jar covered with brightly colored macaroni. The two dollars bought pencils and erasers. . . .

"In comparison with the bounteous gifts the Father bestows upon us—life, the Atonement, the gospel, prophets, scriptures, temples—our gifts to him are like jars covered with macaroni. It's the best we can do, and he accepts our efforts with pleasure. The realization of the difference between us and Him produces deep humility and blessedness." (S. Michael Wilcox, "The Beatitudes—Pathway to the Savior," *Ensign*, January 1991, p. 20.)

Better to Humble Ourselves

"Yea, he that truly humbleth himself, and repenteth of his sins, and endureth to the end, the same shall be blessed—yea, much more blessed than they who are compelled to be humble because of their exceeding poverty.

"Therefore, blessed are they who humble themselves without being compelled to be humble." (Alma 32:15-16.)

Tithing

How Should Tithing Be Calculated?

"When you are in doubt as to just how you should calculate your tithes, reverse the terms . . . and suppose for the time being that the Lord had said this . . . : 'In order to show my love for my people, the faithful members of my Church, it is my will, saith the Lord, that each one shall receive from my storehouse, the storehouse of my church, at regular intervals during the year, an amount equal to one-tenth of his income.' Now my dear brother, sit down and calculate how much the Lord owes you under that kind of law, and then go pay it to your bishop." (James E. Talmage, in Conference Report, October 1928, p. 119.)

Spiritual Prosperity Accompanies the Payment of Tithing

"Prosperity come to those who observe the law of tithing; and when I say prosperity I am not thinking of it in terms of dollars and cents alone. . . . What I count as real prosperity, as the one thing of all others that is of great value to every man and woman living, is the growth in a knowledge of God, and in a testimony, and in the power to live the gospel and to inspire our families to do the same. That is prosperity of the truest kind." (Heber J. Grant, in Conference Report, April 1925, p. 10.)

Saved Her Tithing for Twenty-three Years

"On Sunday, June 26, the first district conference in Hungary was conducted, with fifty-seven people in attendance.

"Among those present was a Hungarian woman who had joined the Church in Germany twenty-three years ago, who has been awaiting the day when the Church would be established in her homeland.

" 'For twenty-three years, she's been putting her tithing in a jar, knowing that one day the Church would come to her and find her,' Elder Nelson said. 'I welcomed her into the church to which she belonged.' " ("News of the Church," *Ensign*, September 1988, p. 75.)

I Will Open the Windows of Heaven

"Will a man rob God? Yet ye have robbed me. But ye say, Wherein have we robbed thee? In tithes and offerings. . . .

"Bring ye all the tithes into the storehouse, that there may be meat in mine house, and prove me now herewith, saith the Lord of hosts, if I will not open you the windows of heaven, and pour you out a blessing, that there shall not be room enough to receive it.

"And I will rebuke the devourer for your sakes, and he shall not destroy the fruits of your ground; neither shall your vine cast her fruit before the time in the field, saith the Lord of hosts." (Malachi 3:8, 10-11.)

6

To every thing there is a season,
and a time to every purpose
under heaven.
—Ecclesiastes 3:1

To Every Thing
There Is a Season

When Janet was twenty-four years old, she had all of the blessings she felt she could handle. She had had her first two children eleven months apart, followed by a miscarriage, and then a beautiful son two years later. So she now cared for a two-year-old daughter, a one-year-old son, and a baby.

One morning, Janet was hurrying around trying to get her three blessings ready to go to daytime Relief Society. The baby was screaming, and the other two little ones were not cooperating. She arrived at Relief Society ten minutes late, put her children in the nursery, and thought to herself, "It will be years before I'll be able to handle another one."

Janet remembers nothing about the lesson that was presented that morning. She does, however, remember letting out a big sigh of relief as she sat down for a blissful, quiet morning with just herself to worry about.

The first thing she heard after the announcements was a friend saying, "Isn't that baby the cutest thing?" They watched in a row ahead of them a tiny baby coo on her mother's shoulder. Janet nodded, not really in the mood to talk about anyone under five feet tall.

Then she heard an audible voice: "It's time for you to have another baby."

She thought to herself, "After my children have gone to bed, when they look so peaceful . . . now that would have been a good time to tell me about having another baby." But the Spirit had definitely whispered, however inappropriate the time. Janet argued with the Spirit throughout the meeting, pointing out her physical and emotional condition. But to no avail. She went out of Relief Society, knowing she was going to have another baby.

Nine months later, a beautiful daughter was born to Janet and her husband.

Six months after her daughter's birth, Janet found out why she so urgently needed to have another baby. It was then that Janet was stricken with severe physical problems. As the weeks of recovery stretched into months, Janet knew it would have been a long time, if ever, before that little daughter could have come to their family. She was grateful for the strong prompting of the Spirit that led her to have her little one safely in her arms before her health problems developed.

Revelation Through the Holy Ghost

The Spirit of Revelation

"Yea, behold, I will tell you in your mind and in your heart, by the Holy Ghost, which shall come upon you and which shall dwell in your heart.

"Now, behold, this is the spirit of revelation; behold, this is the spirit by which Moses brought the children of Israel through the Red Sea on dry ground." (D&C 8:2-3.)

The Holy Ghost Gives Us Foresight

"Would you like to possess perfect foresight, perfected anticipatory powers? If so, you must do as Nephi directed:

'Enter in by the way, and receive the Holy Ghost, [for] it will show unto you all things what ye should do' (2 Nephi 32:5).

"I was touched deeply by an experience that President Thomas S. Monson shared with me. He told of visiting a stake, as a member of the Council of the Twelve, for the purpose of dividing it. As the conference started, he was prompted to inquire concerning the welfare of a former stake president, a man advanced in years. Elder Monson requested that the man be invited to sit on the stand and participate in the program. During the services several speakers felt impressed to pay tribute to this former stake president, acknowledging all he had done to build the Church in that area. Moreover, Elder Monson invited the man to assist in setting apart the newly sustained officers at the close of the conference.

"That night the former stake president commented to his wife that the day had been one of the happiest of his life. A few hours later, the man passed away. What a blessing that President Monson was living close to the Lord! His foresight and anticipatory powers blessed the lives of many through this spiritual experience, including one whose mortal life was closing." (Carlos E. Asay, "The Companionship of the Holy Ghost," *Ensign*, April 1988, p. 16.)

The Holy Ghost Will Teach You What to Do

"In the marvelous experience of Brigham Young in February of 1847, when the Prophet Joseph appeared to him in a dream or vision, Brigham pleaded to be reunited with the Prophet. Brigham Young asked the Prophet if he had a message for the Brethren. The Prophet said:

" 'Tell the people to be humble and faithful, and to be sure to keep the spirit of the Lord and it will lead them right. Be careful and not turn away the still small voice; it will teach them what to do and where to go; it will yield the fruits of the kingdom. Tell the Brethren to keep their hearts open to conviction, so that when the Holy Ghost comes to them, their hearts will be ready to receive it.' " (James E. Faust, "The Gift of the Holy Ghost—A Sure Compass," *Ensign*, May 1989, p. 33.)

Trust in the Lord

Lean Not unto Thine Own Understanding

"Trust in the Lord with all thine heart; and lean not unto thine own understanding.

"In all thy ways acknowledge him, and he shall direct thy paths." (Proverbs 3:5-6.)

Turn to the Lord and Trust Him Through Revelation

"To turn to the Lord and to trust him through revelation will help any individual, at any time, in any part of the world, understand and interpret correctly and righteously life's experiences from the only true perspective, which is the Lord's perspective revealed to man. To turn to the Lord and to trust his revelations is to live in such a way as to resist the floods and the winds of doubt and uncertainty." (Charles Didier, "Spiritual Security," *Ensign*, May 1987, p. 27.)

7

And I saw another angel fly in the midst of heaven, having the everlasting gospel to preach unto them that dwell on the earth, and to every nation, kindred, and tongue, and people.
—Revelation 14:6

Russian People Respond to the Gospel

During the summer of 1990, a group of young people and adults from Utah had the opportunity to spend several weeks in Russia. Many significant changes were to take place in that area of the world not long after the group's visit, including, for example, official recognition of the Church by the Republic of Russia in May 1991, and the dissolution of the Soviet Union in the latter part of 1991. The experiences of these people from Utah demonstrate that the Lord was working on the hearts of the Russian people.

The group was made up of thirty-nine high school students and eleven adult leaders. Included in this number were Layne and Mary and their three children. All but three of the members of the group were Latter-day Saints. A highlight of the trip for the students was the three weeks they spent in Siberia studying Russian language, literature, art, and history. They studied at the university in Akademgorodok, the math and science center for all of what used to be known as the USSR. Mary recorded the following spiritual experiences associated with the trip:

"The Russian people are some of the warmest and most generous people we have ever met. They have so little, but are willing to give so much. We discovered that we had much in common—specifically their love of music, dance, and games. We were the only ones who took our whole family, which intrigued them. We received many invitations to go as a family into our teachers' and Russian friends' homes, and we were pleasantly surprised to see how clean and pleasant their own little apartments were.

"During our stay we had many discussions about the Church. Our sponsors wanted each student to visit a Russian home and to experience their kind of life. In almost all cases, the visits turned to discussions about the beliefs and principles of the Church.

"Several of our students were invited into the home of a couple with two little boys. Hearing that one of the children, Alexander (Sasha) Stupakof, was quite ill, our youth took the opportunity to initiate a gospel discussion by explaining priesthood blessings and the healing of the sick. The young couple anxiously requested that Sasha receive a blessing. The students came and asked that Layne and a friend give the boy a blessing. Before giving the blessing, the group held a short discussion about priesthood blessings and the importance of faith if the blessing was to be beneficial. The group had a prayer together to ask for faith and for the Spirit of the Lord to be there.

"During the blessing, Layne promised the boy that he would sleep well and be completely recovered in the morning. Layne also received strong impressions that this boy would be a great individual in building the Lord's kingdom in Russia.

"The next morning, the boy woke up restored to health. The second son had been kept out of the house to avoid the illness. However, he came down with the fever the next day. The parents again asked for a priesthood blessing, and by the next morning he was healed. Word spread rapidly about these miracles. People asked Layne how men could make someone better by placing their hands on his head. This gave him the opportunity to explain about the priesthood, and that it was not them, but Heavenly Father, who healed the boys.

"Our fifty-member group was given permission to hold our

own sacrament meetings while on this trip. The meetings at Akademgorodok were held in their auditorium and were always attended by Russians. The first Sunday, only a few teachers and several university students were in attendance. The contingent grew each Sunday, and by the third Sunday there were about thirty or forty Russians present. Needless to say, these meetings were full of spirit and emotion, as homesick travelers spoke of their homeland and the blessings of the gospel.

"Many of our Russian teachers and friends commented on the spirit that they felt, but none was touched more deeply than our Russian literature teacher, Raisa Solovjova. Raisa had a beautiful experience that she humbly shared with us. In slow and faltering English, she told us how she had somewhat resentfully accepted the invitation to come to our meeting. She kept asking herself why she should just come to our meeting and be an observer. She thought it was strange that we could hold a religious meeting in 'just any place,' without a real church. She reported that she did not initially understand why she felt compelled to attend, but she did so in spite of her reservations. Raisa reported that, as she sat toward the back of the auditorium, she saw an aura of light hovering over and around the group. It was at this moment, she said, that she knew that 'God was with us.'

"She went on to say that she had learned something important about our character, and then said something that we considered quite profound. She said that she had discovered that 'you carry your faith in your hearts—wherever you go. This is why you do not need a church to worship in. You have something very special and very important, and our people need it so badly.' This sensitive woman went on to thank each of us, and our group as a whole, again and again, for the experience that she had as a result of our visit.

"Since our trip to Russia, Raisa has had the opportunity to accompany a group of Soviet students to the United States. Towards the end of her three-month stay in Massachusetts, some of the students from our group flew Raisa to Utah for our group's reunion. Not only did she attend and speak at the reunion, but she also lectured at junior and senior high schools and at Brigham Young University.

"Our family invited Raisa into our home for dinner on Sunday evening, the day before her return to the East Coast. Raisa shared with us that the faculty and staff of the summer school had been so impressed with our youth that they would like to have more groups of primarily LDS students return, versus groups they had traditionally hosted in the past.

"Now back to Akademgorodok and our experiences there. Layne was placed in a class with a teacher who spoke little English but very good French. Layne had gone to France on his mission, so he served as the translator in the class. The teacher invited Layne to attend a French club meeting that was associated with the university. He went as a guest speaker. The format was very informal. At the beginning of the meeting, he mentioned he was from Utah. Their first question was, 'Aren't there many Mormons in Utah?' Answer, yes. The second was, 'Are you a Mormon?' Layne answered yes. The third was, 'Tell us about your church.' He spent the next two hours speaking in French to eight people, telling them about the Church. Every time he changed the subject, for fear of overstepping his bounds, they would bring the topic back. They are thirsting for the truth.

"Word spread about our group and about the Church. The day before leaving, Layne was stopped on the street by two young men. They asked if he had a few minutes to talk. When he said he had a couple of minutes, the boys asked to hear about the Church. It was the first time Layne had ever been 'golden questioned' by the investigators. They spent over an hour talking about the plan of salvation, the Articles of Faith, the Book of Mormon, and other gospel topics.

"Layne was invited to be the guest speaker for the closing assembly for summer school. After much fasting and prayer, Layne delivered a message to a few hundred Russian students and faculty. He was concerned about the amount of religion he should include in the message. He decided to mix in a good deal, associated with our history and way of life. He discussed the process of sending missionaries. He talked about our roots in Europe and about the pioneers crossing the plains. He talked about the hardships of the missionaries and the struggles they had, and related them to the current struggles in the Soviet

Union. He then discussed what kept them going and quoted 'Come, Come, Ye Saints,' which had a great impact on them.

"After his talk, we discovered that he had not gone far enough. A panel of six of our youth was put up on the stage and asked questions. The first question was 'What don't you like about Russia?' The rest were questions about the Church and how it affects our lives.

"Group members had been told that they could take copies of the Book of Mormon into Russia, but that there was no guarantee that they would not be confiscated at one point or another. Most of our group took at least one copy of the Book of Mormon with a personal testimony and picture inside the front cover. There were many opportunities to place the books—so many that we had to be very selective about the individuals we chose to leave them with, in the hope that they themselves would share them. The group as a whole placed forty-two copies.

"Our family placed eight books and then canvassed our group, trying to find any extra books. We ended up leaving one of our personal quadruple combination books with a very interested professor. All recipients were very touched with the gift. One of the dearest friends we made, Sergei, a twenty-one-year-old student at the Moscow Technical Institute, was reading the book when we left. Our last conversation with him, on the bus heading to the airport, was on the Book of Mormon and the gospel and how, in the near future, young men much like him would be coming to the USSR to teach the gospel to the Soviets.

"The impact of sending forty-seven members of the Church into this area was very great. When the missionaries are sent to Akademgorodok, they will find people waiting to join the Church. There are entire families who have seeds of faith planted in their hearts. This field is truly white and ready to harvest."

Gospel to Every Nation

Nothing Will Stop the Spread of the Gospel

" . . . No unhallowed hand can stop the work from

progressing; persecutions may rage, mobs may combine, armies may assemble, calumny may defame, but the truth of God will go forth boldly, nobly, and independent, till it has penetrated every continent, visited every clime, swept every country and sounded in every ear, till the purposes of God shall be accomplished, and the Great Jehovah shall say the work is done" (Joseph Smith, *History of the Church* 4:540).

All Nations to Receive Gospel Before End Comes

"And this gospel of the kingdom shall be preached in all the world for a witness unto all nations; and then shall the end come" (Matthew 24:14).

Gospel Will Go to Every Nation, Kindred, Tongue, and People

"And I saw another angel fly in the midst of heaven, having the everlasting gospel to preach unto them that dwell on the earth, and to every nation, and kindred, and tongue, and people" (Revelation 14:6).

Member-Missionary Work

Life Is a Mission

"The reason President McKay's pronouncement, 'Every member a missionary,' hits such a responsive and long-lasting chord in the Church and our lives is that it restates a basic eternal truth. We are indeed all missionaries—either for good or for bad, but missionaries nonetheless.

"We must stop trying to separate missionary work from life. Missionary work is life—living is a mission; life is a mission; we are all on a lifelong mission. Our mission on this earth ends only when our life on this earth ends. (Actually, missionary work is forever because life is forever.)

"Thus, it is not a question of whether or not we want to be missionaries. We have already decided that issue. We are alive;

we are here; we are members. The only question is: What kind of missionaries will we be?" (John H. Groberg, "Life Is a Mission," *Ensign*, July 1980, p. 9.)

Arise and Shine

"The Lord has admonished us to 'arise and shine' and be a 'standard to the nations' (see D&C 115:5). He said, 'Let your light so shine before men, that they may see your good works, and glorify your Father which is in heaven' (Matthew 5:16). Yes, the Lord intends that we be a light to the world." (Ezra Taft Benson, *The Teachings of Ezra Taft Benson* [Salt Lake City: Bookcraft, 1988], p. 329.)

The World Is Ready for the Gospel

"Never have we had the opportunity which we have today to get our message before the world. Almost all over the world the Church is well-spoken of. Never has it been so easy to get a gospel conversation. Never has the Christian world been weaker than it is today. Never has there been a need, such a great need, for what we have. We must share the gospel with others. That is our responsibility—every member a missionary. That is the call of prophets of God." (Ezra Taft Benson, *The Teachings of Ezra Taft Benson*, p. 208.)

8

Now they were desirous that salvation should be declared to every creature, for they could not bear that any human soul should perish; yea, even the very thoughts that any soul should endure endless torment did cause them to quake and tremble.
—Mosiah 28:3

Don't Worry About Him

When President Prescott called Brother Evans to be a bishop, he issued several challenges. One of the challenges was to increase the number of families being home taught. Another was to increase sacrament meeting attendance.

Bishop Evans worked out a plan to meet these challenges. He decided that more effective home teaching would be the best way to increase sacrament meeting attendance. He worked closely with the priesthood leaders over several months. Each leader followed up with interviews and personal visits. During this concerted effort, many lives were touched. Over ninety percent of the families were visited regularly during several months. This success with the home teaching had a direct effect on sacrament meeting attendance, which rose from percentages in the mid-twenties to the sixties. As this success was recognized, Bishop Evans and the other leaders were elated.

As time went on, they seemed to reach a plateau with the sacrament meeting attendance. They just could not rise above the sixties. But they were satisfied that they had done all they needed to, and they conceded that the sixties was a lot better than the twenties.

Bishop Evans always looked forward to stake conference. It was like a vacation to him. He had no ward meetings to worry about, and he could sit with his young family during the meeting. His wife especially enjoyed having help with their three little ones.

After one particular stake conference, Bishop Evans was taught a great lesson. As people were leaving, Sister Evans stopped to visit with one of the ward members. Bishop Evans had their youngest child in his arms and the other two by his side. As he waited for his wife, their oldest son, who was three, slipped away unnoticed into the crowd. When Bishop Evans noticed he was missing, he frantically looked through the crowd for him. As he made his way through the crowd, he was stopped by President Prescott. The stake president, seeing the distressed look on his face, asked Bishop Evans what was wrong. Bishop Evans indicated that his oldest son was missing.

President Prescott then asked, "How many children do you have?"

Bishop Evans replied, "Three."

President Prescott then said, "Let's see . . . you have two with you. That's over sixty percent. . . . Don't worry about him."

The stake president was obviously trying to teach the bishop a lesson. Bishop Evans was able finally to locate his son, and this experience caused him to take a new look at what was being done to "reach the one" in the ward, regardless of what the percentages were. This new perspective helped him to see ways to reach some of the so-called "unreachables." As these ideas were implemented, the ward climbed to a new plateau.

The Worth of a Soul

Remember the Worth of Souls Is Great

"Remember the worth of souls is great in the sight of God. . . .

"And if it so be that you should labor all your days in crying repentance unto this people, and bring, save it be one soul unto me, how great shall be your joy with him in the kingdom of my Father!

"And now, if your joy will be great with one soul that you have brought unto me into the kingdom of my Father, how great will be your joy if you should bring many souls unto me!" (D&C 18:10, 15-16.)

The Lord's Purpose Is to Save Individuals

" . . . We are not saved as congregations, nor as groups, but we are saved as we come into the world as individuals, and the Lord's purpose is to save the individual, each being precious in his sight" (David O. McKay, "Salvation, an Individual Responsibility," *Improvement Era*, June 1957, p. 389).

Magnify Callings

Lengthen Our Stride

"So much depends upon our willingness to make up our minds, collectively and individually, that present levels of performance are not acceptable, either to ourselves or to the Lord. In saying that, I am not calling for flashy, temporary differences in our performance levels, but a quiet resolve . . . to do a better job, to lengthen our stride." (Spencer W. Kimball, *The Teachings of Spencer W. Kimball*, ed. Edward L. Kimball [Salt Lake City: Bookcraft, 1982], p. 174.)

Life Is a Competition with Ourselves

"Life is a competition not with others, but with ourselves. We should seek each day to live stronger, better, truer lives; each day to master some weakness of yesterday; each day to repair a mistake; each day to surpass ourselves." (David B. Haight, "The Responsibility of Young Aaronic Priesthood Bearers," *Ensign*, May 1981, p. 42.)

Gospel Living Is a Process

"Gospel living is a process of continuous individual renewal and improvement until the person is prepared and qualified to enter comfortably and with confidence into the presence of God" (Ronald E. Poelman, "The Gospel and the Church," *Ensign*, November 1984, p. 65).

Let Every Man Learn His Duty

"Wherefore, now let every man learn his duty, and to act in the office in which he is appointed, in all diligence.

"He that is slothful shall not be counted worthy to stand, and he that learns not his duty and shows himself not approved shall not be counted worthy to stand." (D&C 107: 99-100.)

9

Sing, O heavens; and be joyful, O earth; and
break forth into singing, O mountains: for
the Lord hath comforted his people, and will
have mercy upon his afflicted.
—Isaiah 49:13

It Was
Broken

It was New Year's Eve, and Kenny had run over to his father's house for a few minutes. The phone rang. It was his wife, Jenny, asking him to come home because there had been an accident.

When Kenny arrived home, he found out that Austin, their five-month-old baby, had fallen onto his face. Jenny had put Austin in his baby seat and set it on the kitchen counter so that she could feed him. As Jenny turned around to get his food, her young daughter had come into the kitchen. She wanted to see the baby better, so she pulled his seat closer to her. This caused the seat and the baby to slip off the counter. Austin was strapped into the seat, and he landed, face down, on the kitchen floor, with the seat on top of him.

When Jenny first picked him up, he was screaming at the top of his lungs, but she could not see anything wrong with him. She sat down in the living room with the baby on her lap, and he continued to scream. She realized that that kind of screaming meant he must be really hurting. She looked a little closer. As Austin took a deep breath to get more air for his screams, Jenny saw that his two new teeth were bent straight toward the back of his mouth. That is when she called Ken and told him to hurry home.

When Ken and his uncle gave Austin a blessing, he quieted right down. They then rushed him to the local hospital. After examining him and taking X rays, the doctor said that his jaw was broken and that there was nothing they could do there to help him. He added that the teeth might not grow in properly because of the severity of the blow to his mouth and jaw. The doctor said that he would need to be taken to Primary Children's Hospital in order to receive the care he needed.

When they called Primary Children's Hospital, they were told that the doctor on call could not help them and that, it being New Year's Eve, they could not locate a specialist. The best they could do was set up an appointment for the next morning at eight o'clock.

As Kenny and Jenny left the local hospital, they felt sick inside. But there was little they could do other than take Austin home and wait until morning. When they arrived home, they knelt down and pleaded with Heavenly Father that he would bless Austin so that there would be no permanent damage. Both of them felt the Spirit very strongly as they finished their prayer.

When they went to the hospital the next morning, they took the X rays with them and gave them to the doctor. He took the X rays into the next room and soon returned with the confirmation that the X rays showed a broken jaw. The doctor then took Austin into the next room to examine him. He returned in a few minutes and said that he could not feel anything out of line. He said that when he poked Austin's jaw it did not seem to hurt him, and that Austin did not seem to be in any kind of pain.

He suggested that Austin be X-rayed again to find out what was going on. He returned with the news that he could see where Austin's jaw had been broken, but that it was completely healed. He went on to say that everything seemed to be lined up perfectly and that he expected Austin to suffer no problem with his teeth coming in properly. Kenny and Jenny's sincere prayer had been answered in a miraculous way.

Miracles

Miracles Beyond Imagination Happen Today

"A question often asked is: If miracles are a part of the gospel program, why do we not have such today?

"The answer is a simple one: We do have miracles today— beyond imagination! If all the miracles of our own lifetime were recorded, it would take many library shelves to hold the books which would contain them.

"What kinds of miracles do we have? All kinds—revelations, visions, tongues, healings, special guidance and direction, evil spirits cast out. Where are they recorded? In the records of the Church, in journals, in news and magazine articles and in the minds and memories of many people." (Spencer W. Kimball, *The Teachings of Spencer W. Kimball*, ed. Edward L. Kimball [Salt Lake City: Bookcraft, 1982], p. 499.)

God Is a God of Miracles

"For behold, I am God; and I am a God of miracles; and I will show unto the world that I am the same yesterday, today, and forever; and I work not among the children of men save it be according to their faith" (2 Nephi 27:23).

Miracles Are Shown to All Those Who Believe

"For I am God, and mine arm is not shortened; and I will show miracles, signs, and wonders, unto all those who believe on my name.

"And whoso shall ask it in my name in faith, they shall cast out devils; they shall heal the sick; they shall cause the blind to receive their sight, and the deaf to hear, and the dumb to speak, and the lame to walk." (D&C 35:8-9.)

Prayer

Nothing Centers Our Attention on God More than Prayer

"There is nothing in the gospel that is better designed to keep the attention of men centered on God, on righteousness, and on their duties than is prayer. Every thought, word, and act is influenced or governed by the nature and extent of one's communion through prayer with Deity." (Bruce R. McConkie, *Mormon Doctrine*, 2d ed. [Salt Lake City: Bookcraft, 1966], p. 581.)

Great Spiritual Treasures Can Be Obtained Through Prayer

"Pray always, and I will pour out my Spirit upon you, and great shall be your blessing—yea, even more than if you should obtain treasures of earth and corruptibleness to the extent thereof.

"Behold, canst thou read this without rejoicing and lifting up thy heart for gladness?" (D&C 19:38-39.)

Unity Important When Praying

"And, as it is written—Whatsoever ye shall ask in faith, being united in prayer according to my command, ye shall receive" (D&C 29:6).

Priesthood Blessings

How Important Is the Faith of the Person Receiving the Blessing?

"The need of faith is often underestimated. The ill one and the family often seem to depend wholly on the power of the priesthood and the gift of healing that they hope the administering brethren may have, whereas the greater responsibility is with him who is blessed. There are persons who seem to have the gift to heal, . . . but after all, the major element is the faith of the individual when that person is conscious and account-able. 'Thy faith hath made thee whole' was repeated so often by the Master that it almost became a chorus. Though he was the Redeemer and 'all power is given me in heaven and in earth,' yet his oft-repeated statement was, *'Thy faith hath made thee whole.'"* (Spencer W. Kimball, "Administration to the Sick," *New Era*, October 1981, p. 47.)

Should We Seek Medical Attention After Receiving a Blessing?

"Some have charged us with inconsistency, for they say: 'If you believe in the gift of healing, what is the need of doctors, what is the need of surgeons, why build hospitals?' Because we know that 'there is a law irrevocably decreed in heaven, before the world was, and when we attain any blessing it is by obedience to that law upon which it is predicated;' and the law is, in the instance under consideration, that we shall do all we can of ourselves. . . .

"We must do all we can, and then ask the Lord to do the rest, such as we cannot do. Hence we hold the medical and surgical profession in high regard. . . . When we have done all we can then the Divine Power will be directly applicable and operative." (James E. Talmage, from a 1921 address, quoted in "Viewpoint," *Church News*, 19 February 1977, p. 16.)

Commanded to Seek Priesthood Blessings

"Is any sick among you? let him call for the elders of the church; and let them pray over him, anointing him with oil in the name of the Lord:

"And the prayer of faith shall save the sick, and the Lord shall raise him up; and if he have committed sins, they shall be forgiven him." (James 5:14-15.)

10

*Be thou humble; and the Lord
thy God shall lead thee by the
hand, and give thee answer
to thy prayers.
—D&C 112:10*

Visit
Sister Smith

Elder Stephens and Elder Carl, missionaries, were on a bus headed to the other side of town. All of a sudden they both had a feeling that they needed to stop and visit Sister Smith.

Neither one of them understood why they should change their plans. Sister Smith was not expecting them and there was no reason to visit her. But they knew that they should heed a prompting that had come with such strength to both of them. So, as the bus got to the street where Sister Smith lived, they got off of the bus and went to her home.

To their surprise and disappointment, Sister Smith wasn't home. They were confused. Why would they both be prompted to visit Sister Smith, if she wasn't even going to be home?

They caught another bus and went to the other side of town, where they had been going in the first place.

Later they learned that the bus that they had been riding on first had been in an accident. Then they understood. Heavenly Father had seen the big picture. In order to protect them, he had prompted them in a way that would get them to leave the bus that was going to crash. They were grateful for a loving Father who had kept them safe that day.

The Love and Wisdom of God

God Sees and Hears All

"There are no corners so dark, no deserts so uninhabited, no canyons so remote, no automobiles so hidden, no homes so tight and shut in but that the all-seeing One can penetrate and observe. The faithful have always known this. The doubters should take a sober look at the situation in the light of the electronic devices which have come into increasing use in the last few years and which are often delicate and tiny but so powerful as almost to annihilate man's personal privacy. . . .

"In the light of these modern marvels can anyone doubt that God hears prayers and discerns secret thoughts? A printer's camera can make a negative three feet square. What magnification! If human eyes and ears can so penetrate one's personal life, what may we expect from perfected men with perfected vision!" (Spencer W. Kimball, *The Miracle of Forgiveness* [Salt Lake City: Bookcraft, 1969], pp. 110-11.)

Divine Guidance

The Lord Shall Guide Thee

"And the Lord shall guide thee continually, and satisfy thy soul in drought, and make fat thy bones: and thou shalt be like a watered garden, and like a spring of water, whose waters fail not" (Isaiah 58:11).

God Shall Lead Thee by the Hand

"Be thou humble; and the Lord thy God shall lead thee by the hand, and give thee answer to thy prayers" (D&C 112:10).

Led by the Spirit

"And I was led by the Spirit, not knowing beforehand the things which I should do" (1 Nephi 4:6).

I Will Lead You Along

"And ye cannot bear all things now; nevertheless, be of good cheer, for I will lead you along" (D&C 78:18).

He Leadeth Thee by the Way

"Thus saith the Lord, thy Redeemer, the Holy One of Israel; I am the Lord thy God which teacheth thee to profit, which leadeth thee by the way that thou shouldest go" (Isaiah 48:17).

Directions Where They Should Travel

"And it came to pass that the Lord commanded them that they should go forth into the wilderness, yea, into that quarter where there never had man been. And it came to pass that the Lord did go before them, and did talk with them as he stood in a cloud, and gave directions whither they should travel." (Ether 2:5.)

11

*That thy glory may rest down upon thy people,
and upon this thy house, which we now
dedicate to thee, that it may be sanctified
and consecrated to be holy, and that thy holy
presence may be continually in this house.*
—*D&C 109:12*

A Heavenly Choir

Don and his wife served as custodians of their local chapel. During the winter they had to get a fire going in the old chapel stove by five o'clock on Sunday mornings in order for the building to be warm enough for the nine o'clock priesthood meeting.

On one such morning, long before the sun came up, they pulled on their warm clothes and climbed into their car. Even though the morning was cold, it was so bright and beautiful that they didn't even bother to turn the car headlights on. As they drove slowly through the magnificent winter panorama, they could hear the ice crystals crunching under the wheels of the car.

They coasted up to the front of the chapel and stopped the car. When they turned the key off, they could hear singing coming from the church. A choir was singing a hymn familiar to both Don and his wife. They listened to the music for a while and commented on how beautiful it was. All of a sudden his wife said, "Hey, there's not supposed to be anybody in there."

They both got out of the car and walked quietly toward the chapel. As they walked they could still hear the singing. When they reached the front door, his wife told Don to wait a few minutes before entering, until she could run around to the back door. After waiting for her to reach the other door, Don got out his keys and unlocked the front door. As soon as he touched the door, the music stopped. When he entered the chapel and turned the lights on, he found that the chapel was empty. About this time his wife came in from the back, having seen no one leave.

Don shared this experience with his bishop and with others, and said that he never cleaned the building again without feeling that his job was a special one. He was convinced that the chapel was in use much more than the ward members realized. He was so grateful that the Lord had allowed him to listen through the veil and hear the angels sing.

Dedicated Buildings

All Church Buildings Belong to the Lord

"I would like to explain something about a dedication. You have all contributed to this building and in a sense it belongs to you right now. You have some 'ownership' of it. Someone paid for the ceiling tile, for the carpet, the glass, the curtains, the wood paneling, the shelves, and the chairs; but in just a few minutes, I am going to act as your agent to turn this building over to the Lord.

"By so doing, we each relinquish our ownership of the building. . . . In dedicating a building, we present it officially as our gift to the Lord. This means that tomorrow morning when anyone enters this building, *they are here as guests of the Lord*. It then belongs to Him. That places tremendous responsibility upon the brethren—our teachers here. They are under serious responsibility to maintain the building as beautiful and appealing as it can be made. They are under responsibility to have a spirit here in the building that is completely worthy of the ownership of the building; and they are under the necessity of maintaining order among the students in such a way that there will be no disrespect either in conduct, thought, or action toward the purpose for which this building was erected." (Boyd K. Packer, Spanish Fork Seminary dedication services, Spanish Fork, Utah, 29 August 1962.)

Temples Are Sanctified

"That thy glory may rest down upon thy people, and upon this thy house, which we now dedicate to thee, that it may be sanctified and consecrated to be holy, and that thy holy presence may be continually in this house;

"And that all people who shall enter upon the threshold of the Lord's house may feel thy power and feel constrained to acknowledge that thou hast sanctified it, and that it is thy house, a place of thy holiness." (D&C 109:12-13.)

Angels

Angels Watch Over Us

" . . . During my travels in the southern country last winter I had many interviews with President Young, and with Heber C. Kimball, and Geo. A. Smith, and Jedediah M. Grant, and many others who are dead. They attended our conference, they attended our meetings. . . . I believe myself that these men who have died and gone into the spirit world had this mission left with them, that is, a certain portion of them, to watch over the Latter-day Saints." (Wilford Woodruff, in *Journal of Discourses* 21:318.)

Righteous Loved Ones Continue to Influence Us

" . . . Our fathers and mothers, brothers, sisters and friends who have passed away from this earth, having been faithful, and worthy to enjoy these rights and privileges, may have a mission given them to visit their relatives and friends upon the earth again, bringing from the divine Presence messages of love, of warning, or reproof and instruction, to those whom they had learned to love in the flesh." (Joseph F. Smith, *Gospel Doctrine* [Salt Lake City: Deseret Book Co., 1939], p. 436.)

Angels Singing and Praising God

"And being thus overcome with the Spirit, he was carried away in a vision, even that he saw the heavens open, and he thought he saw God sitting upon his throne, surrounded with numberless concourses of angels in the attitude of singing and praising their God" (1 Nephi 1:8).

Music

Music Can Soothe and Inspire

"Throughout the ages music has inspired men with hope, given voice to their joys, kindled their love, and soothed them in times of despair. So often if affects us in ways that we find difficult to explain. At times it becomes a communication of spirit that need not be articulated to be understood and can lead us to moments when we seem to touch the infinite." (Wilma Boyle Bunker, "The Value of Music in My Life," *Ensign*, March 1971, p. 30.)

Importance of Selecting Our Music Carefully

"Through music, man's ability to express himself extends beyond the limits of the spoken language in both subtlety and power. Music can be used to exalt and inspire or to carry messages of degradation and destruction. It is therefore important that as Latter-day Saints we at all times apply the principles of the gospel and seek the guidance of the Spirit in selecting the music with which we surround ourselves." (First Presidency, *Priesthood Bulletin*, August 1973.)

Song Can Be Prayer to God

"For my soul delighteth in the song of the heart; yea, the song of the righteous is a prayer unto me, and it shall be answered with a blessing upon their heads" (D&C 25:12).

Praise the Lord with Song

"If thou art merry, praise the Lord with singing, with music, with dancing, and with a prayer of praise and thanksgiving" (D&C 136:28).

12

*And now, I, Moroni, would speak somewhat concerning
these things; I would show unto the world that faith is
things which are hoped for and not seen; wherefore,
dispute not because ye see not, for ye receive no witness
until after the trial of your faith.*

—Ether 12:6

Don't Worry—
It's Me

One afternoon Elder Bird and Elder Dubon, missionary companions in Guatemala, were looking at their agendas. They noticed that they had a very important appointment that could result in five baptisms. They were to meet with a family of seven who lived way above the little town of Palo Gordo.

They had visited this family before and had had a lot of success in teaching them the gospel. They had always visited them in the daytime, never at night, because their home was so far away and because of the problems with the rebels, a group of people opposed to the government of Guatemala. The rebels would often go out at night to stir up trouble, stealing chickens and other things.

This time, however, because the family could not meet with them during the day, the missionaries ended up with an eight o'clock evening appointment with this family that meant so much to them. They decided to leave for the appointment at about 6:00 P.M., hoping to get there at about 7:00 P.M., just before it got dark. Before they left they both knelt and prayed that the Lord would bless the family and bless the missionaries to travel safely.

They made it safely to the house before dark and started to teach the family. They had a good discussion, and the family accepted the challenge to be baptized the next Sunday. The discussion ended about 9:00 P.M.

The missionaries were a little afraid to head down the mountain. They had no flashlight and there was no other light for miles. But they had faith that the Lord would help them find their way down without their being bothered by the rebels. However, as they started down the hill, they wandered off the small trail, and were soon lost in the dark. They had no idea where to go, so they looked around for a few minutes, hoping to hear someone or see something that could help them.

Unable to find help, their fear increased. They knew the rebels were always in the mountains at night, so they kept quiet and just hoped they could figure out what to do. After a while they decided that the only way out would be with the Lord's help. They both knelt down to say a prayer. They each prayed vocally, taking turns, both asking for help to get out safely. After both of them prayed, they got up, looked around, and decided to go down the hill a little farther. It didn't help; they found themselves even more lost than before.

At this point they decided to kneel down one more time and really pray with lots of faith, knowing that they would receive an answer this time. They both knelt down; this time, they felt their prayers were more sincere than before. As they got up, they still felt lost and very scared; but they hoped for an answer to their prayers. They looked around again, wondering where to go and what to do. Then they heard a noise coming toward them. They were very frightened, but they knew the Lord would protect them. As the noise got closer, they could tell it was a person coming toward them. As the person got close to them, he spoke out and called them by name, saying, "Elders, don't worry. It's me."

It was the branch president. He said that he had been sitting at home when he heard a voice telling him that the missionaries were in trouble and that they needed help. So he left the house to find them. He didn't know where to look, so he just began to walk; and the Spirit guided him right to them.

Elder Bird and Elder Dubon were glad to see him and glad to make it home safely. From that time on, they knew that the Lord really does answer prayers when we are willing to pray with all our might and strength.

Faith and Prayer

Whatsoever Ye Shall Ask in Faith

"And, as it is written—Whatsoever ye shall ask in faith, being united in prayer according to my command, ye shall receive" (D&C 29:6).

Obtain This Blessing by Diligence

"And it is my will that you shall humble yourselves before me, and obtain this blessing by your diligence and humility and the prayer of faith" (D&C 104:79).

Exercise Fervent Prayer and Faith

"And now, brethren, after your tribulations, if you do these things, and exercise fervent prayer and faith in the sight of God always, he shall give unto you knowledge by His Holy Spirit, yea by the unspeakable gift of the Holy Ghost, that has not been revealed since the world was until now" (Joseph Smith, *Teachings of the Prophet Joseph Smith*, sel. Joseph Fielding Smith [Salt Lake City: Deseret Book Co., 1938], p. 138).

Earnest Prayer Consists of Feeling from the Heart

"I pray you, my young brethren who are present in this vast congregation, and who are liable to be called to preach the gospel to the world, when you are called to go out, I pray that you will know how to approach God in prayer. It is not such a difficult thing to learn how to pray. It is not the words we use particularly that constitute prayer. Prayer does not consist of words, altogether. True, faithful, earnest prayer consists more in the feeling that rises from the heart and from the inward desire of our spirits to supplicate the Lord in humility and in faith, that we may receive his blessings. It matters not how simple the words may be, if our desires are genuine and we come before the Lord with a broken heart and contrite spirit to ask him for that which we need." (Joseph F. Smith, *Gospel Doctrine* [Salt Lake City: Deseret Book Co., 1939], p. 219.)

We Should Call upon the Lord in Mighty Prayer

" . . . I fear, as a people, we do not pray enough in faith. We should call upon the Lord in mighty prayer, and make all our wants known unto him. For if he does not protect and deliver us and save us, no other power will." (Wilford Woodruff, *Discourses of Wilford Woodruff*, sel. G. Homer Durham [Salt Lake City: Bookcraft, 1969], p. 221.)

Prayer Is a Great Boon

"Prayer in the hour of need is a great boon. From simple trials to our Gethsemanes, prayer can put us in touch with God, our greatest source of comfort and counsel." (Ezra Taft Benson, *The Teachings of Ezra Taft Benson* [Salt Lake City: Bookcraft, 1988], p. 432.)

13

*And remember in all things the poor
and the needy, the sick and the
afflicted, for he that doeth not these
things, the same is not my disciple.*
—D&C 52:40

Please Ask Them
to Come Again

Very few things bring the Spirit of the Lord into our lives faster and more abundantly than giving service to others. A group of teenagers learned this great truth as they served together on a seminary council. Most release-time seminaries have a student council that plans the activities for the year. Seminary teachers usually take turns serving as the adviser to the council. This particular year it was Brother Ashby's turn to serve.

One of the students on the council, Becky, was responsible for planning all of the sacrament meeting programs the seminary would give. These included the sacrament meeting programs at the local rest home, which were to be given by the seminary on the first Sunday of each month throughout the year.

Becky approached Brother Ashby and told him that she felt that they should not assign others to go to the rest home, but that the council, including Brother Ashby as the adviser, should present those sacrament meeting programs. Brother Ashby was quite hesitant about this idea because he felt that he ought to be attending sacrament meetings in his home ward and fulfilling his other responsibilities. He really didn't like the idea of committing himself to twelve more meetings.

Becky was very persistent and said that she really felt strongly that this was something the seminary council should do together as a group. Brother Ashby didn't know what else to do, so he finally said that they would give it a try.

As Brother Ashby sat in the rest home during the council's first sacrament meeting program, he received a strong impression that he and the students, before they left, should shake the hand of every patient who had attended the meeting. He communicated this to the students, and after the meeting they shook each person's hand.

When the council returned a month later for their second sacrament meeting, the whole room was filled with people. At least three times as many people were there than on the previous occasion. Brother Ashby asked one of the rest home staff why so many had come. She said that it was because the patients had so loved their previous visit.

This time, about halfway through the talks, the Spirit of the Lord came so strongly that everyone began to cry. Once again, when the meeting was over, council members went around and shook everyone's hand.

When they came to the rest home the third time, the room was packed again. As Brother Ashby concluded his talk, he was directed by the Spirit to ask one of the girls who had just spoken to stand up again and bear her testimony. She hadn't borne her testimony during her talk. She bore such a powerful testimony that the room was again immersed in the Spirit of God. She later told Brother Ashby that this was the first time she had ever borne her testimony, and that, during her testimony, she realized for the first time that she really knew the Church was true.

After the students had shaken hands with everyone in the room, one of the nurses commented that she had never seen her patients want a group of people to return as much as they did this group of young people. She said that they were the only group of people that the patients had ever requested back again, and she mentioned that they never had this kind of attendance at their other sacrament meetings. Even patients who usually said little or nothing had asked for these seminary students to return. They said it was because the patients could hear the students when they spoke, and because they especially loved to visit with them afterwards.

Their last meeting at this rest home, at the end of the school year, was one of the most inspirational meetings Brother Ashby had ever attended. He had never felt the Spirit stronger than he did at that meeting. Every student knew it would be their last time to be there together, and the spirit of love and unity was overwhelming.

One of the council members later wrote to Brother Ashby from the mission field. He said that the opportunity to serve on the council that year was the highlight of all of his high school experiences. He had been on the basketball team and involved in several student offices, but nothing that he had done in high school brought feelings comparable to the joy and satisfaction that had come to him as he had served his Father in Heaven and his fellowmen.

Service

Service Brings Joy and Gladness

" . . . We must surely realize that there can be no true worship of Him who is the Christ without giving of ourselves. . . .

"If we will give such service, our days will be filled with joy and gladness. More important, they will be consecrated to our Lord and Savior, Jesus Christ, and to the blessing of all whose lives we touch." (Gordon B. Hinckley, "Giving Ourselves to the Service of the Lord," *Ensign*, March 1987, p. 5.)

We Serve God by Serving Others

"And behold, I tell you these things that ye may learn wisdom; that ye may learn that when ye are in the service of your fellow beings ye are only in the service of your God" (Mosiah 2:17).

We Have Promised to Bear One Another's Burdens

"And it came to pass that he said unto them: Behold, here are the waters of Mormon (for thus were they called) and now, as ye are desirous to come into the fold of God, and to be called his people, and are willing to bear one another's burdens, that they may be light;

"Yea, and are willing to mourn with those that mourn; yea, and comfort those that stand in need of comfort, . . .

" . . . what have you against being baptized in the name of the Lord?" (Mosiah 18:8-10.)

Discipleship Includes Remembering Those in Need

"And remember in all things the poor and the needy, the sick and the afflicted, for he that doeth not these things, the same is not my disciple" (D&C 52:40).

14

*And whatsoever ye shall ask the Father
in my name, which is right, believing that
ye shall receive, behold it shall be given
unto you.*
—3 Nephi 18:20

Peanuts

Many children have a great deal of faith and trust in Heavenly Father. They are not afraid to ask for blessings, and, many times, they fully expect to receive them. From the time that he was very young, Ryan demonstrated this kind of faith.

When Ryan was ten years old, his favorite horse became very ill. She was an old mare that they called Peanuts, and he had come to really love her. Ryan's family loaded the horse into a trailer and took her to the city to a veterinarian. He told them that the old mare had a serious blockage and that nothing really could be done for her. He sadly explained that the horse would probably have to be destroyed the next morning.

The family had brought Ryan with them, and when he heard this news, it nearly broke his heart. The horse he loved the most—the one that had become his best friend—was going to be destroyed. The veterinarian went on to explain that he would try several things during the rest of the day, but he felt that none of them would work and that the horse would have to be put down the following morning.

When the family returned home, Ryan asked if he could go over to his cousin's house. The parents were not surprised at this. He had always been the kind of boy who would try to keep busy when things were going bad so that he would not have to think about them. They assumed he wanted to play with cousins Larry and Reese.

Playing, however, was not what Ryan had in mind. When he arrived at Larry and Reese's house, he told them that Peanuts was really sick and that the veterinarian was going to have to put her to sleep. He asked his cousins if they would go into the bedroom and kneel down with him to pray for Peanuts. The boys were willing. They knelt down together and asked Heavenly Father to heal Peanuts and make her okay.

Ryan's family knew nothing about the prayer that had been offered by these three faithful boys. When Ryan's father called the veterinarian the next morning, fully expecting to find that the horse had been put to sleep, he found that this was not the case. The veterinarian said that, much to his surprise, the horse was doing much better. He told Ryan's dad that they would give the horse a little more time. He said he could not believe the difference in the horse. They would know later in the day if the improvement was lasting, so Ryan's dad should call again that evening.

When the father called that night, the veterinarian told him to come and get Peanuts—she was fine. He said that he had no idea how the horse had made it through the night or why she had recovered.

Ryan's family had no idea why the horse had recovered either, because Ryan had not told them about the prayer he and his cousins had offered to God.

A day or two later, the cousins' mother called Ryan's mother. She had overheard the three boys asking Heavenly Father to bless the old horse, and she had been amazed at their faith. This was how Ryan's family found out about the miracle that had been performed in behalf of Peanuts. As old as she was, Peanuts lived for several more years. This was a testimony to the three boys, and to their families, of the strength of prayer.

Ryan also demonstrated faith that includes humility and

appreciation. As soon as he heard that Peanuts had been healed, he went into his bedroom, got down on his knees, and thanked his Heavenly Father.

The Faith of a Child

Children Often Strengthen Their Parents

A seven-year-old girl, Jamie, was one of seven children who had fasted and prayed for their mother who had been battling cancer for a year. Along with their father, they had prayed that their mother would be healed; but after three especially difficult months, she had passed away.

The father gathered his children together to pray, and then sent them to their rooms to get ready for bed. Jamie had been close to her mother and had loved her very much, yet she felt no resentment toward the Lord. She knelt down at the side of her bed and, through her tears, she prayed, "Heavenly Father, we thank thee for the great mom you gave us. We thank thee for helping us try to make her well. Help us to be good so we can live with her again." What a strength this must have been to her father! (Retold by authors from address by Michaelene P. Grassli, "Children at Peace," *Ensign*, November 1988, p. 78.)

We Need to Humble Ourselves as Children

" . . . Verily I say unto you, Except ye be converted, and become as little children, ye shall not enter into the kingdom of heaven.

"Whosoever therefore shall humble himself as this little child, the same is greatest in the kingdom of heaven." (Matthew 18:3-4.)

Of Such Is the Kingdom of Heaven

"But Jesus said, Suffer little children, and forbid them not, to come unto me: for of such is the kingdom of heaven" (Matthew 19:14).

Saints Develop Many Childlike Qualities

" . . . [He] putteth off the natural man and becometh a saint through the atonement of Christ the Lord, and becometh as a child, submissive, meek, humble, patient, full of love, willing to submit to all things which the Lord seeth fit to inflict upon him, even as a child doth submit to his father" (Mosiah 3:19).

Prayer

Many Prayers Are Too Self-Centered

"Even in our prayers, our words are mostly *gimme*— 'Father, *make* us strong, *give* us health, *make* us righteous'— when we should be thanking him mostly and asking only for help in our doing these things for ourselves" (Spencer W. Kimball, *The Teachings of Spencer W. Kimball*, ed. Edward L. Kimball [Salt Lake City: Bookcraft, 1982], p. 120).

Talk with, *Not* to, *Heavenly Father*

"When you pray—when you talk to your Heavenly Father—do you really talk out your problems with Him? Do you let Him know your feelings, your doubts, your insecurities, you joys, your deepest desires? Or is prayer merely a habitual expression with the same words and phrases? Do you ponder what you really mean to say? Do you take time to listen to the promptings of the Spirit? Answers to prayer come most often by a still voice and are discerned by our deepest, innermost feelings. I tell you that you can know the will of God concerning yourselves if you will take the time to pray and to listen." (Ezra Taft Benson, *The Teachings of Ezra Taft Benson* [Salt Lake City: Bookcraft, 1988], p. 428.)

Humility a Necessary Ingredient in Prayer

"Be thou humble; and the Lord thy God shall lead thee by the hand, and give thee answer to thy prayers" (D&C 112:10).

God Wants to Bless Us

"And whatsoever ye shall ask the Father in my name, which is right, believing that ye shall receive, behold it shall be given unto you" (3 Nephi 18:20).

15

Nevertheless they did fast and pray oft, and did wax stronger and stronger in their humility, and firmer and firmer in the faith of Christ, unto the filling their souls with joy and consolation, yea, even to the purifying and the sanctification of their hearts, which sanctification cometh because of their yielding their hearts unto God.
—Helaman 3:35

Yielding Her Heart unto God

K arie had prayed all of her life that she would never be left as a widow. Because she had lost her mother when she was just a little girl, she dearly wanted her own children to have both a mother and a father to love and nurture them. Daily in her prayers, she asked her Heavenly Father to please give her children the blessing of having both parents.

She and her husband, Lloyd, had been married about eleven years when Lloyd experienced his first heart attack. It was a massive heart attack, and he lay in the hospital with very little hope that he would recover. Karie pleaded for him in prayer. The whisperings of the Spirit came to her mind, and she felt the assurance come that she would not be left a widow. Heavenly Father answered her prayers and allowed Lloyd to stay.

During the following year Lloyd became active in the Church. He was ordained an elder, and he and Karie went to the temple and were sealed as a family for time and eternity.

Seven good years passed, and then, once again, Karie was

faced with the frightening possibility of losing her mate. Lloyd had another serious heart attack.

Lloyd came through this heart attack also, but it left him with damage to his heart which required open heart surgery. This took place three months later. The surgery went very well; so well, in fact, that shortly after his surgery, he was taken out of intensive care. But for some unknown reason, he went into cardiac arrest. For the next twenty-five minutes Lloyd's spirit visited the spirit world. The hospital personnel worked feverishly on him, although they felt that they would probably never be able to revive him.

During this twenty-five minutes, Karie was wrestling with the Lord. She told him that she did not want him to take Lloyd. She told him that there was no way that she would let her husband go. And Lloyd's condition just kept getting worse.

The doctors came to Karie and told her that they needed to perform a particular procedure. They didn't know if it would work, but they felt it was the last chance they had to try to save him. Karie signed the consent papers, and then left the waiting room and went for a walk.

She found a secluded place in the hospital and poured out her heart and soul to the Lord. For the first time, she bowed her will to his. She told him that she couldn't imagine living without Lloyd, but she knew that God's will must be done. She finally realized that it was Heavenly Father's decision, not hers; and that if Lloyd's life was to be spared, it could only be by God's hand. She told him that if he was going to take Lloyd, she would really need His help so that she could accept and understand her loss. Then she released Lloyd into Heavenly Father's care.

The most peaceful, comforting spirit embraced her. She felt the Lord put his arms around her and give her renewed strength and faith. Then she returned to the waiting room where her family and friends were. As she went down the hall, she could see the doctor coming towards her, shaking his head. Her heart sank, for she thought that he was going to tell her that Lloyd was gone. Instead, the doctor said, "I don't know what's going on, but his numbers are starting to come up, and he is improving. We are not going to do the procedure right now."

At that moment Karie knew that, before Heavenly Father performed his miracle, he had wanted her to be willing to release Lloyd and to place her trust in Him. There was no loud trumpet, no rolling of drums, no fireworks. There was just a calm, peaceful feeling that assured her that the Lord had saved her husband's life again.

Miracles happen. They happen every day. But before they can come, we must exercise our faith and our hope in Heavenly Father and his wisdom, and place our trust in him.

Faith and Hope

We Can Reach for Hope

" . . . The daily work of the Lord involves changing hopeless to hopeful—for all of us. And it is for us to find at last that in the midst of winter we have within us an invincible summer. In a world filled with adversity we can reach for joy." (Elaine Cannon, "Reach for Joy," *Ensign*, May 1982, p. 95.)

Do Not Depend on Your Own Strength Alone

"In life . . . you should seek the help you need. Do not depend on your own strength alone. You have never done all you can to finish a task until you have sought help from the Lord." (Joseph B. Wirthlin, "Running Your Marathon," *Ensign*, November 1989, p. 74.)

There Is No Witness Until After a Trial of Our Faith

"And now, I, Moroni, would speak somewhat concerning these things; I would show unto the world that faith is things which are hoped for and not seen; wherefore, dispute not because ye see not, for ye receive no witness until after the trial of your faith" (Ether 12:6).

Miracles

All Things Are Possible to Them That Believe

"Miracles belong to no particular time or place. Wherever and whenever there is a legitimate demand for the exercise of divine power, that power will act, and marvels will result. We worship a God of miracles, and he changeth not, but is the same yesterday, today and forever (Mormon 9:7-11, 17-20). There is but one valid reason for the absence of miracles among any people, and that is the absence of faith. 'All things are possible to them that believe.'" (Orson F. Whitney, in Conference Report, April 1925, p. 22.)

Our Setbacks Will Be But a Moment

"We will all have disappointments and discouragements—that is part of life. But if we will have faith, our setbacks will be but a moment and success will come out of our seeming failures. Our Heavenly Father can accomplish miracles through each of us if we will but place our confidence and trust in Him." (Ezra Taft Benson, *The Teachings of Ezra Taft Benson* [Salt Lake City: Bookcraft, 1988], p. 68.)

16

He Needed Long-Sleeved Cotton Shirts

Michael received a call to serve a mission in Argentina. While shopping for his mission clothes, he and his mother disagreed on the type of shirts he should purchase. The mother wanted him to buy polyester so that he wouldn't need to iron them. She also felt that they looked very dressy. Michael, however, insisted that he could only take long-sleeved cotton shirts. When his mother questioned him about this, he replied, "I don't really know why they must be cotton. I just have these strong impressions that this is important." This ended the discussion, and they bought the cotton shirts.

Months later, Michael had an experience that demonstrated to him why the Lord inspired him to purchase the shirts that he did. While knocking on doors, Michael and his companion met a lady who invited them into her home without even finding out who they were. At first the missionaries thought that she must either be an inactive member or someone who just wanted to argue religion. They discovered she was a person who was truly interested in learning more about the truth. They taught her a lesson, very successfully, and made an appointment to return.

They were running late for another appointment, so they didn't finish knocking doors on the rest of the street. Later that day, during lunch, an elderly lady showed up at the lunchroom where the missionaries were eating. She found Michael and asked him why he hadn't come to her house to teach her. She said that she had been waiting for him. It turned out that she was the other woman's neighbor, living in one of the homes they hadn't reached. When she said that it was very important that they come, they made an appointment to see her the following Thursday. When Michael started to shake hands with her, she grabbed his hands and kissed them.

The woman's name was Antonia. When they stopped by her house on Thursday, the woman was not home. Usually the missionaries would stop only once in a day at someone's house; if the person was not at home, they would try again another day. The Spirit, however, kept telling them to go back to Antonia's house. After returning several times, they finally found her home. She had been to see her doctor, and had worried the whole time she was gone that she would miss the missionaries. She said that she had prayed all morning that they wouldn't give up. She had something important to tell them.

After they were seated in her home, she told them of a dream she had experienced over twenty years before. At that time in her life she had been very depressed and had lost her desire to continue living. In one year she had lost her mother to a heart attack, lost her husband in an auto accident, and lost her home and all of her worldly belongings. All that remained was her faith in God, and that was dwindling rapidly.

One night, Antonia offered her last plea for help and went to bed. While she was sleeping, she saw a fair-skinned young man, dressed in a white, long-sleeved cotton shirt. She ran to him and dropped to her knees. She begged him to show her the way. He comforted her and told her to be patient and wait because he would come to her and help her find her way. When he turned to leave, she ran after him and caught him just as he was entering a garden gate. He turned to her and said again, "Be patient; I'm coming."

That was the end of her dream, but she awakened with a peace that she hadn't felt for a very long time. She had spent the next twenty years waiting and searching for the fair-skinned young man in the white, long-sleeved cotton shirt.

Antonia then said that three weeks ago she had seen the man from her dream getting on a bus in the city of Carlos Pass. Before she could get to the bus, it had pulled away. She felt devastated. But then she read the sign on the bus, her devastation turned to joy, for it was headed to the very town she lived in. Standing there in the street, she had vowed that she would find him. Two weeks later she had seen him again with another young man. This time they were riding bikes and were soon lost to her view. She knew again that this young man was the one from her dream and prayed that God would help her find him.

On the morning that Michael and his companion had called on her neighbor, she had been out in her yard pulling weeds. They had gone inside her neighbor's house and hadn't come out for a long time. She had waited and waited as long as she could, but finally she had to leave. When she returned, she had gone to the neighbor and asked who the young men were and where she could find them.

The neighbor had told her that they were Mormon missionaries and that they normally ate lunch between noon and one o'clock in the dining hall on the street named Sacramento. When she found them, she singled out Michael and kissed his hands because he was the young man in her dream. By the time she finished telling her story, she and the missionaries were in tears, and Michael was in shock.

That afternoon Michael and his companion taught Antonia about the plan of salvation, and gave her a copy of the Book of Mormon. She was so excited to learn the truth! She reminded them that she had waited more than twenty years to hear what they were telling her.

This experience had a great impact on Michael. He wrote in his journal, "I have never felt such an outpouring of the Spirit in my entire life. At my farewell, I told the congregation that I was going to find my eternal friend (as in the play *Star Child*). Well, it turns out that my eternal friend's name is Antonia.

"Tonight I feel so happy, so complete, that I could die this moment and have no regrets. One of the really thrilling things about this story is that it was *me* she dreamed about—not Mormon missionaries, not my companion, but *me*. Then a sobering, even a frightening, thought hit me. What if I had chosen not to serve my Heavenly Father on a mission? Perhaps Antonia would have missed her chance at the gospel.

"I was transferred before Antonia was baptized, but I'll always be thankful that I was able to bring her the joy and happiness of the gospel of Jesus Christ."

Revelation Through Dreams

Some Dreams Are Revelations from God

"Now there's one more way by which revelations may come, and that is by dreams. Oh, I'm not going to tell you that every dream you have is a direct revelation from the Lord—it may be fried liver and onions that have been responsible for an upset or disorder. But I fear that in this age of sophistication there are those of us who are prone to rule out all dreams as of no purpose, and of no moment. And yet all through the scriptures there were recorded incidents where the Lord, by dreams, has directed His people. . . .

"When we begin to understand that beyond sight, as Brigham Young said, the spirit world is right here round about us, and if our spiritual eyes could be open, we could see others visiting with us, directing us. And if we will learn not to be so sophisticated that we rule out that possibility of impressions from those who are beyond sight, then we too may have a dream that may direct us as a revelation." (Harold B. Lee, *Stand Ye in Holy Places* [Salt Lake City: Deseret Book Co., 1974], pp. 142, 143.)

Sometimes the Lord Directs Us Through Dreams

"The Lord has revealed to men by dreams something more than I ever understood or felt before. I heard this more than once in quorum meetings of the Council of the Twelve when George F. Richards was president. He was the venerable father of Brother LeGrand Richards who has just spoken to us. He said, 'I believe in dreams, brethren. The Lord has given me dreams which to me are just as real and as much from God as was the dream of King Nebuchadnezzar, which was the means of saving a nation from starvation, or the dream of Lehi who through a dream led his colony out of the old country across the mighty deep to this promised land, or any other dreams that we might read in the scriptures. It is not out of place for us to have important dreams.'" (Spencer W. Kimball, "The Cause Is Just and Worthy," *Ensign*, May 1974, p. 119.)

There Will Be Dreams and Visions in the Last Days

"And it shall come to pass afterward, that I will pour out my spirit upon all flesh; and your sons and your daughters shall prophesy, your old men shall dream dreams, your young men shall see visions" (Joel 2:28).

Inspiration

Obedience Increases Inspiration

"I know some people who will say, 'How can I conduct my life so as to be responsive to the message that comes from an unseen world?' There's an old illustration that bears on this subject: We may take a rod of iron and place it with some filings without apparently causing any change—the rod is not magnetic. But if we wrap that rod with a wire carrying an electric current, it becomes a magnet. Though the rod has not changed in shape and width and length, it has undergone a deep change. It has become changed so that it attracts iron filings or whatever else is subject to magnetic action. Just so, if each of us could wrap ourselves in obedience to God's love and live as we should, a wonderful change would be effected in us, and we too could then hear the messages from the unseen world." (Harold B. Lee, *Stand Ye In Holy Places*, p. 135.)

How to Receive Personal Revelation

"Would you like the formula to tell how to get personal revelation? It might be written in many ways. My formula is simply this:
1. Search the scriptures.
2. Keep the commandments.
3. Ask in faith.

(Bruce R. McConkie, "How to Get Personal Revelation," *New Era*, June 1980, p. 50.)

The Spirit Will Show Us Things to Come

"Howbeit when he, the Spirit of truth, is come, he will guide you into all truth: for he shall not speak of himself; but whatsoever he shall hear, that shall he speak: and he will shew you things to come" (John 16:13).

17

And he shall turn the heart of the fathers to the children, and the heart of the children to their fathers.
—Malachi 4:6

Let's Say a Little Prayer

Sylvia was born in Baltimore, Maryland, but has lived for some time in Kona, Hawaii. Several years ago she was working on her genealogy and ran into a snag. Several dates were missing, and none of her family on the mainland had the information.

Sylvia and her husband had planned a trip to Baltimore to visit her sister and brother. She had been gone from there for twenty-six years, and she looked forward to the visit.

While in Baltimore, she felt a strong desire to visit her mother's grave. Her mother was buried in the little town of Rosedale, in the suburbs. Sylvia's sister told them how to get to the cemetery and that it was called Rosedale.

When Sylvia was last in Baltimore, there had been only two small cemeteries. Now there were cemeteries on both sides of the road as far as the eye could see.

They parked the car and walked up the road, looking for Rosedale Cemetery. But they had no success. Finally Sylvia said to her husband, "Let's go back to the car and say a little prayer." They went back to the car and, while sitting inside the car, they asked the Lord to help them. Then they got out of the car and again walked up the road. On the other side of the street, farther up, they saw some men digging a grave. Walking up to them, Sylvia inquired if they knew where the Rosedale Cemetery was. One of the men asked, "Which one—Rosedale Progressive or Rosedale Hebrew?"

She replied, shaking her head, "I don't know."

He then asked whom she was looking for. She told him, "The grave of my mother, Minnie Paul."

He replied, "Oh! I know where she is buried. I took your uncle to her grave sixteen years ago."

With that, he proceeded to lead Sylvia and her husband back across the road and into one of the cemeteries. He led them directly to her mother's grave. Nearby were the graves of her mother's brother and her grandmother. There, on the headstones, was some of the information she needed.

Sylvia and her husband had rented a video camera. They asked the man if they could take his picture. He said he didn't have time, as he had work to do. He indicated that if she needed information about her father's brother, the path in the center of the cemetery would lead her to his grave.

With this he turned and walked away. Sylvia's husband was getting the camera out of the case and turned around to take the man's picture, but he was gone.

They followed his directions and found her uncle's grave along with his wife's grave. They also found her Aunt Rebecca's grave and her father's mother's grave. There on the tombstones was the rest of the information she needed to complete her family group sheets.

The help that Sylvia received that day strengthened her testimony that, once a family has done what they can do, the Lord will assist them in their genealogy work.

Genealogy

The Lord Will Provide Ways

" . . . While we do the work for our dead ancestors, we will reach a limit after a while. That limit will be after we have gone as far as records are kept. I have said that when any man or woman goes into this work earnestly the Lord will provide ways and means for them to obtain the information they seek. Our understanding will be opened and sources of knowledge will be made manifest. Why? Because the dead know a great deal more than we do about existing records." (Melvin J. Ballard, *Three Degrees of Glory*, address delivered in the Ogden Tabernacle, 22 September 1922 [Salt Lake City: Joseph Lyon and Associates, 1975], p. 23.)

We Cannot Fail If We Do Our Part

"In this work we cannot fail if we do our part. The Lord will not permit us to fail. This is His work. He will open the doors in our genealogical research. He will bless us as we come to the temple. No, we cannot fail." (Ezra Taft Benson, *The Teachings of Ezra Taft Benson* [Salt Lake City: Bookcraft, 1988], p. 163.)

Help from the Spirit World

" . . . My grandfather, being one of a family, searched all his life to get together his genealogical records; and when he died, in 1868, he had been unsuccessful in establishing his line back more than the second generation beyond him. I am sure that most of my family members feel the same as I do—that there was a thin veil between him and the earth, after he had gone to the other side, and that which he was unable to do as a mortal he perhaps was able to do after he had gone into eternity. After he passed away, the spirit of research took hold of men—his family in the West and two distant relatives, not members of the Church, in the East. For seven years these two men—Morrison and Sharples—unknown to each other, and unknown to the members of the family in the West, were gathering genealogy. After seven years, they happened to meet and then for three years they worked together. The family feels definitely that the spirit of Elijah was at work on the other side and that our grandfather had been able to inspire men on this side to search out these records; and as a result, two large volumes are in our possession with about seventeen thousand names." (Spencer W. Kimball, *The Teachings of Spencer W. Kimball*, ed. Edward L. Kimball [Salt Lake City: Bookcraft, 1982], p. 543.)

A Way Will Be Opened

"The Lord expects of us all that we do what we can for ourselves and for our dead. He wants us to make the search for our ancestry because he does not do for us what we can do for ourselves. And after we have done all we can, then means will be furnished, or the way will be opened for the finishing of the information which we are unable to discover." (Joseph Fielding Smith, *Doctrines of Salvation*, comp. Bruce R. McConkie, 3 vols. [Salt Lake City: Bookcraft, 1954-56], 2:149.)

The Lord Will Help Us Get the Job Done

"The Lord is in this work. He wants it to prosper. He wants us to be successful in our efforts. While living with my grandmother, Louise Ballif Benson, in Logan as a student, I knew she had been working very hard on her research. She kept referring to the fact that there was a gap that she couldn't fill and it worried her. She prayed about it fervently. One day she received a package addressed just 'Benson Family, Utah.' The package contained a printed book which had come from a man in Syracuse, New York, who had done research independently—not as a member of the Church. You can imagine the joy that filled my grandmother's heart when she found that this not only filled the gap, but did much more than that. Her prayers had been answered. Yes, there are many ways to help get the job done." (Ezra Taft Benson, *Teachings of Ezra Taft Benson*, p. 164.)

18

*. . . As ye are desirous to come into the fold of God,
and to be called his people, . . . and to stand as witnesses
of God at all times and in all things, and in all places
that ye may be in, even until death, . . . what have you
against being baptized in the name of the Lord?*
—Mosiah 18:8-10

Standing Up for the Right

The Church was building a new chapel in a small isolated town in Utah. Kenneth's company bid for the job and was given the contract. Kenneth was assigned to be foreman. Because of the distance involved, Kenneth and his family decided to temporarily move their home to this small town, until the chapel was completed. This would keep the family together.

Kenneth was responsible not only for making sure the work met the requirements of the blueprints and specifications, but also for directing and overseeing the workers. Sometimes this could be a difficult job. Construction workers are not always mild mannered and soft spoken. Members and nonmembers alike work on these building sites, and working hours may be the only time that some of these workmen are found within the confines of a chapel.

The Church has a policy that once a chapel has been framed in, no tobacco should be used within the building. Most of the workers think of cigarette smoking in regard to this policy, and they go outside the building to smoke. Kenneth had the responsibility of enforcing this policy and other policies that the Church had set.

In the construction of this particular chapel, Kenneth ended up with an especially difficult crew to work with. They were extremely foul mouthed, and two of them chewed tobacco constantly and spit their juice all over the subfloor of the chapel. Kenneth talked to them several times about their language and tried, in a kind way, to get them to treat the building site with some respect. He realized that the chapel had not yet been completed or dedicated, but it still bothered him to hear some of their language and to find tobacco juice everywhere.

He finally had a serious discussion with them. He underlined the fact that they were building a church, and told them that some of the things they were doing needed to be stopped immediately. Most of the men seemed to respond positively to this, but one young man seemed more rebellious than the rest. This particular young man had a serious chewing problem, and he continued to spit on the chapel subfloor.

One day Kenneth decided that he had cleaned up tobacco juice for the last time. He sought out this young man and reminded him of the Church policy concerning tobacco within a framed building. The young man replied that the policy only referred to smoking and commented that he could chew tobacco as much as he wanted. When Kenneth said that there would be no more chewing in his church, the young man replied that he would continue to chew and Kenneth couldn't stop him.

Finally Kenneth told him that he would kick him off the job if he didn't quit chewing tobacco in the building. The young man finally realized Kenneth was serious, and he gave up tobacco chewing while on the job. Within a few days the men became much more cooperative; some of them even became quite friendly.

Since this community was fairly isolated, this particular crew stayed in town and worked twelve-hour days from Monday through Thursday. They would then go home to their families over the three-day weekend. This meant that they were usually working or sleeping during the four days they were in town.

When their portion of the job was finished, which took about six months, the young man who had given Kenneth a rough time approached him and apologized to him for the way he had acted at the beginning of the job. He then told Kenneth that he wanted to thank him for helping him to kick a filthy habit, one that he had been trying to kick for years. He thanked Kenneth for having the courage to stand up to him and tell him what was right, even though he had made it difficult. Not being able to chew four days out of the week had given him the help he needed to quit chewing the other three days. He said that he had not chewed tobacco for over two months, and shared with Kenneth how happy this had made his wife.

Kenneth learned a great lesson that day. Standing up to this particular young man had been difficult and unpleasant, but a life had been changed. It strengthened his resolve to stand up for the right, no matter what situation he might find himself in.

Moral Courage

Courage Begins with a Personal Decision

"We live in one of the most critical periods of all time. The powers of evil are fighting against truth and righteousness, and the battle is reaching a climax. Someday the war between good and evil will be won—a permanent victory for good. But right now each one of you can fight for the right on your own battlefield by making right choices about what you will do and what you won't do as you learn to listen to the promptings of the Spirit. Once you make your decision to do what is right, you don't have to fight the battle with every temptation that presents itself every day. You simply take a stand and say to yourself, 'I will do this; I won't do that.' And Satan will have to turn elsewhere to find his followers." (Ardeth G. Kapp, "Stand for Truth and Righteousness," *Ensign*, November 1988, p. 94.)

Courage Is Needed to Make Life's Decisions

"Life's journey is not traveled on a freeway devoid of obstacles, pitfalls, and snares. Rather, it is a pathway marked by forks and turnings. Decisions are constantly before us. To make them wisely, courage is needed: the courage to say *no*, the courage to say *yes*. Decisions do determine destiny." (Thomas S. Monson, "Courage Counts," *Ensign* November 1986, p. 40.)

Joseph Smith Displayed Great Moral Courage

"So it was with me. I had actually seen a light, and in the midst of that light I saw two Personages, and they did in reality speak to me; and though I was hated and persecuted for saying that I had seen a vision, yet it was true; and while they were persecuting me, reviling me, and speaking all manner of evil against me falsely for so saying, I was led to say in my heart: Why persecute me for telling the truth? I have actually seen a vision; and who am I that I can withstand God, or why does the world think to make me deny what I have actually seen? For I had seen a vision; I knew it, and I knew that God knew it, and I could not deny it, neither dared I do it; at least I knew that by so doing I would offend God, and come under condemnation." (Joseph Smith—History 1:25.)

We Promise to Stand Up for God When We Are Baptized

"And it came to pass that he said unto them: Behold, here are the waters of Mormon (for thus were they called) and now, as ye are desirous to come into the fold of God, and to be called his people, and are willing . . .

" . . . to stand as witnesses of God at all times and in all things, and in all places that ye may be in, even until death, that ye may be redeemed of God, and be numbered with those of the first resurrection, that ye may have eternal life—

"Now I say unto you, if this be the desire of your hearts, what have you against being baptized in the name of the Lord?" (Mosiah 18:8-10.)

19

---

*. . . By small and simple things are great things brought to pass. . . .
And the Lord God doth work by means to bring about his great
and eternal purposes; and by very small means the Lord doth
confound the wise and bringeth about the salvation of many souls.*
—Alma 37:6-7

The Very
Night

Scott was getting ready to go home teaching when his telephone rang. The bishop was on the other end of the line and, coincidentally, wanted to speak to Scott about home teaching. He said that there was a young widow in the ward who really needed some help. She had four children she was trying to raise by herself, and things had not been going very well for her. The bishop acknowledged that Scott had his own assigned families to visit, but wondered if he could visit this widow until they could assign regular home teachers to her.

Scott indicated that he would be glad to visit her, then left to pick up his companion. They visited one of their assigned families and then dropped by the widow's home. When they rang the door bell, no one answered. They could hear children yelling and screaming, and decided that the noise had drowned out the sound of the bell. So they rang again. Again there was no response. But on the third ring, the woman answered the door.

The woman's hair was a mess and her house was in total

disorder. She was very hesitant about letting them come in, but she finally invited them to come in and sit down. The children were still running around, and Scott could tell that she had been crying. He told her that the bishop had asked them to come; then they taught a short lesson. After they had talked for a few minutes, they prayed with her and left.

A few weeks later the bishop called Scott again. He had not yet had time to assign a regular home teacher for the woman; he wondered if Scott and his companion would visit her one more month. The bishop said that he had tried himself to visit her several times, but other things had kept him from doing this. Scott indicated that they would be glad to visit her again, and told the bishop not to worry about it.

It was late in the evening when they visited her for the second time, and it was almost a repeat performance of their previous visit. It took three tries before the woman opened the door, and the children were just as noisy as they had been on the previous occasion. The home teachers shared another short message with her and knelt in prayer together. They let her know that they were there to help her in any way they could. She thanked them for coming, and they went home to their families.

By the next month, regular home teachers had been assigned to this woman, so Scott did not visit her again. For the next few months he went about his normal activities and almost forgot about her. Then one Sunday, he and his family were sitting on the front row during fast and testimony meeting. (His family had been late to the meeting, and the front seats are usually the last to go in most Mormon chapels.) Earlier in the meeting he had blessed and named their new baby, and he was now peacefully enjoying the spirit of the meeting. His ward used a portable microphone that was passed around the congregation, and since he was sitting on the front row, those who were bearing their testimonies were behind him. He had enjoyed hearing three or four testimonies. Then someone else started speaking. The voice sounded familiar to him, but he could not identify it. When he turned around to see who it was, he recognized the widow that he and his companion had visited.

She told of the struggle she had faced since losing her husband, and of the problems she had encountered trying to raise her children by herself. She said that a few months ago she had finally reached a point in her life where she felt she could no longer face her problems. She had made the decision to take her own life.

She chose the night this would take place and prepared for it. She paid the bills and made out her will. She wrote a good-bye letter to the children. Everything was prepared, and she only had to get the children into bed before following through on her plans. Then the door bell rang. That was the night of Scott's first visit.

She told how the home teachers had prayed for her and how they had given her a message from the Lord. This made her feel that the Lord was watching over her, and she decided that suicide was not the answer.

She went another month, and then became depressed again. Once again she felt that it was too difficult to go on, and she prepared to take her life. Once again she wrote a letter to her children and made everything ready. And once again the door bell rang, and it was her home teachers. This helped her to realize that the Lord cared about her personally; and the joy of knowing that the Lord loved her sunk deep into her heart.

She then told how the bishop had called her and told her that she now had regular home teachers who would visit her often. The new home teachers had visited her regularly. She then shared with the congregation how her whole outlook on life had changed.

As Scott listened to her words, tears flowed down his cheeks. He had not realized that he had made any difference at all in the life of this sister.

Like most of us, Scott had underestimated the power that comes into people's lives as we quietly and faithfully strive to fulfill our responsibilities in the Church. We may, like Scott, have an occasional glimpse of some good that has come from our actions. But we will have to wait for the next life to truly comprehend how many lives have been affected by simple, loving service in the Church.

Church Service

Loving Service Begins a Chain of Good

"How does one measure the impact of an act of love performed selflessly in another's behalf?

"The answer, of course, is that the results are incalculable.
Such acts never cease once they are performed, because the
person helped then helps others and on it goes. These efforts
literally begin a chain of good that influences first an individual, then perhaps his family, the perhaps a quorum or a ward,
possibly the community, and even generations. So powerful is a
single act of love.

"Such power is not for Apostles alone or bishops or quorum
presidents. Some of life's most important blessings are shared
when we simply do our 'duty with a heart full of song.'" (Giles
H. Florence, Jr., "Links in the Chain of Good," *Ensign*, February
1987, p. 15.)

Church Service Means Bringing People to Christ

"You are called of God to serve His children. You may be
called as a clerk or a home teacher or a visiting teacher. You all
are a son or daughter or a brother or sister. None of those are
accidental calls. And each places you in service to invite someone to choose the right, to come unto Christ. None of the people
for whom you are responsible can be truly served without your
bearing testimony, in some way, of the mission of Jesus Christ."
(Henry B. Eyring, "Come unto Christ," in *Brigham Young University 1989-90 Devotional and Fireside Speeches* [Provo,
Utah: University Publications, 1990], p. 41.)

The Worth of Souls Is Great

"Remember the worth of souls is great in the sight of
God. . . .

"And if it so be that you should labor all your days in crying repentance unto this people, and bring, save it be one soul

unto me, how great shall be your joy with him in the kingdom of my Father!

"And now, if your joy will be great with one soul that you have brought unto me into the kingdom of my Father, how great will be your joy if you should bring many souls unto me!" (D&C 18:10, 15-16.)

Home Teaching

You Were the Hope in My Life

"An LDS girl whose two parents took no part in Church activities later wrote this recollection to an elder who had been her home teacher:

" 'You were the bright hope in my often difficult life. There is no greater call than a home teacher. You loved and showed respect for my parents. You honored them and at the same time supported me. You were *there!* . . . As I look back now, I realize you and the truth you offered were my life-support.

" 'Behind the doors were years of pain, tears, and fear. You were able to come into our home and chase them away, if only for a short time. No one else could do that.' " (Dallin H. Oaks, "Modern Pioneers," *Ensign*, November 1989, p. 67.)

We Visit to Help Parents Become Spiritual Leaders

"We do not visit the active just to 'visit,' or the less active just to get them out to church, although that may be part of what happens. In essence, we visit to help the heads of those homes, male or female, to become the spiritual leaders in their homes, to lead their families to Christ, to pray, to fast, and to read the scriptures together. If that happens in our visits, all else will take care of itself." (Gene R. Cook, "Inviting Others to 'Come unto Christ,' " *Ensign*, November 1988, p. 37.)

Unto What Were Ye Ordained?

"Wherefore, I the Lord ask you this question—unto what were ye ordained?

"To preach my gospel by the Spirit, even the Comforter which was sent forth to teach the truth." (D&C 50:13-14.)

20

And what is it that ye shall hope for?
Behold I say unto you that ye shall have hope
through the atonement of Christ and the power
of his resurrection, to be raised unto life eternal,
and this because of your faith in him according to the promise.
—Moroni 7:41

Hope Replaced
Despair

As they laid her newborn baby next to her on the delivery room table, Launa watched his tiny lungs pull for all they were worth. She could count his ribs. She was a nurse herself and she knew what it meant. She was fairly sure that her baby had hyaline membrane. Her heart was filled with pain. She knew that the death rate for children with that disorder was 98 percent. Her baby would only live by the providence of God.

Her husband, Carl, not realizing the baby was sick, had hurried home to call his relatives and friends and give them the good news. When he got back to the hospital and found out his baby probably would not live through the night, he was shattered.

He returned home to tell his relatives to fast and pray. He then spent the whole night on his knees. He expressed to God how much he loved the child and promised that, if he would allow the child to live, he would try to be a good father to him.

Arriving at the hospital the next morning, Carl was told he had better hurry if he was going to administer to his baby. As

Carl delicately laid his hands on his baby boy's tiny head, he was impressed to bless him to get well and to be able to come home.

The baby improved miraculously and was able to come home with his mother when she was released from the hospital. The doctor was very surprised. He was a specialist, and he had never seen an infant recover from this disease the way this baby did. He indicated that, in the rare cases when a baby did survive, it almost always needed to stay in the hospital for at least two months.

Before the baby was born, Carl and Launa had chosen the name of David, but after the intervention of the Lord they decided to name him John, which means "a gift of God."

For the rest of the story, we quickly skip over several more children and find Launa in the hospital having her seventh child. This time it was a little girl they named Lillian, and she seemed perfect in every way. She was seven-and-a-half pounds and had fat cheeks, black hair, and beautiful eyes.

Just before she was to go home from the hospital, a doctor's examination found that Lillian had a heart murmur. She was immediately sent to Primary Children's Hospital for specialized attention.

Carl remembered how the Lord had blessed them when John was sick. Now he fasted and prayed for another miracle with Lillian. This time, however, when he laid his hands on Lillian's small head and asked permission from the Lord to bless her to get well, the Lord said no. Lillian died that night.

Carl was very troubled by this. As he drove away from the hospital the next morning, tears were streaming down his cheeks. He asked Heavenly Father, "Why?" Why John and not Lillian? Why all the pain?"

Then God did something very special for Carl. He showed him the reunion that he and Launa would have with Lillian. It was so overwhelming that Carl was completely immersed in the joy of that great hope. The feeling and vision and joy of being united again was so special that Carl had no more tears of sadness left.

During those really hard first days and weeks after the baby's death, Carl was able to bless Launa through the priesthood. He was emotionally capable of speaking at Lillian's funeral and dedicating her grave. He was able to perform the many other tasks associated with her death, without stress and without discouragement. Despair was replaced by peace and hope, and both he and Launa received comfort from the Lord.

Salvation of Children

No Blessing Is Withheld from Children Who Die

"Little children shall be saved. They are alive in Christ and shall have eternal life. For them the family unit will continue, and the fulness of exaltation is theirs. No blessing shall be withheld. They shall rise in immortal glory, grow to full maturity, and live forever in the highest heaven of the celestial kingdom—all through the merits and mercy and grace of the Holy Messiah, all because of the atoning sacrifice of Him who died that we might live." (Bruce R. McConkie, "The Salvation of Little Children," *Ensign*, April 1977, p. 3.)

Children Who Die Will Be Raised by Parents During Millennium

"Joseph Smith taught the doctrine that the infant child that was laid away in death would come up in the resurrection as a child; and, pointing to the mother of a lifeless child, he said to her: 'You will have the joy, the pleasure, and satisfaction of nurturing this child, after its resurrection, until it reaches the full stature of its spirit.' . . . I love this truth. It speaks volumes of happiness, of joy and gratitude to my soul." (Joseph F. Smith, *Gospel Doctrine* [Salt Lake City: Deseret Book Co., 1939], pp. 455-56.)

Children Redeemed Through the Atonement

"But behold, I say unto you, that little children are redeemed from the foundation of the world through mine Only Begotten" (D&C 29:46).

Hope, Inner Peace

We Can Enjoy Peace During Times of Strife

"It is a great blessing to have an inner peace, to have an assurance, to have a spirit of serenity and inward calm during times of strife and struggle, during times of sorrow and reverses. It is soul-satisfying to know that God is at the helm, that He is mindful of His children, and that we can with full confidence place our trust in Him." (Ezra Taft Benson, *The Teachings of Ezra Taft Benson* [Salt Lake City: Bookcraft, 1988], p. 68.)

God Speaks Peace to His Saints

"I will hear what God the Lord will speak: for he will speak peace unto his people, and to his saints" (Psalm 85:8).

Let Not Your Heart Be Troubled

"Peace I leave with you, my peace I give unto you: not as the world giveth, give I unto you. Let not your heart be troubled, neither let it be afraid." (John 14:27.)

Resurrection

There Is No Physical Growth in the Grave

"When a baby dies, it goes back into the spirit world, and the spirit assumes its natural form as an adult, for we were all adults before we were born.

"When a child is raised in the resurrection, the spirit will enter the body and the body will be the same size as it was when the child died. It will then *grow after the resurrection* to full maturity to conform to the size of the spirit.

"If parents are righteous, they will have their children after the resurrection. Little children who die, whose parents are not worthy of an exaltation, will be *adopted* into the families of those who are worthy." (Joseph Fielding Smith, *Doctrines of Salvation*, Comp. Bruce R. McConkie, 3 vols. [Salt Lake City: Bookcraft, 1954-56], 2:56.)

Sting of Death Swallowed Up in Christ

"And if Christ had not risen from the dead, or have broken the bands of death that the grave should have no victory, and that death should have no sting, there could have been no resurrection.

"But there is a resurrection, therefore the grave hath no victory, and the sting of death is swallowed up in Christ." (Mosiah 16:7-8.)

All Will Be Resurrected

"The spirit and the body shall be reunited again in its perfect form; both limb and joint shall be restored to its proper frame, even as we now are at this time. . . .

"Now, this restoration shall come to all, both old and young, both bond and free, both male and female, both the wicked and the righteous; and even there shall not so much as a hair of their heads be lost; but every thing shall be restored to its perfect frame." (Alma 11:43-44.)

21

*And again, it is given to some
to speak with tongues.*
—D&C 46:24

The Gift
of Tongues

As Elder Paskett said good-bye to his missionary companion
and watched the train pull out of the station, he had no idea
that he would be without a companion for about three weeks.
On his journey to Elder Paskett's mission area, his new companion had become very ill; he had to be hospitalized. This left
Elder Paskett alone to cope with a difficult and frightening situation.

Shortly after his companion left, a family they had been
friends with was struck with a great tragedy. Their twenty-six-
year-old son became very ill. The son and the father were Latter-day Saints, but the mother and the daughters were devout
Catholics.

The son suffered excruciating pain before the illness took
his life. During his period of suffering, his mother and sisters
told him that God was punishing him for leaving the mother
church. He displayed great courage by bearing his testimony of
the truthfulness of the Church. He told them that he realized
that he was going to die, and he wanted to maintain and cherish

his testimony to the end. He refused to blame God or to waver in his faith, in spite of the pain and suffering he was called upon to endure.

Early one morning, the boy's father knocked on Elder Paskett's door. He asked Elder Paskett to take care of his son's burial. The father was devastated with grief. He wanted someone who represented God's church and priesthood to lay his son's earthly remains away until the morning of the first resurrection when they could be together again. Elder Paskett was the only one in the entire area that the father felt was qualified to take care of his son's burial.

The problem was that Elder Paskett had been in the mission field for only a short time and had not, as yet, developed a fluency in Spanish. (At that time the missionaries received no language instruction before entering the mission field.) To the father, Elder Paskett's ability or non-ability to speak the language was of minor importance. After all, did not Elder Paskett hold the priesthood, and had he not been set apart as a special emissary to administer the gospel to the Lamanites?

With reasoning like this, Elder Paskett found it impossible to say no. As he tried to prepare a funeral sermon, he realized his tremendous language inadequacy. He asked two Church members to accompany him and give their moral support.

When they arrived at the home of the bereaved family, they were invited in. The casket containing the body of the young man was situated in the middle of the room. Three chairs were set up on one side of the casket. This is where Elder Paskett and his two friends were to sit. About two dozen chairs were placed on the other side of the casket. The family and neighbors seated themselves in these chairs and waited expectantly for Elder Paskett to begin.

As he sat there, trying to get the courage to stand, he thought to himself, "What am I going to do?" After silently asking the Lord to help him, he decided that the only thing he could do was to try. As he stood up and began to speak, the Holy Ghost put beautiful Spanish words into his mouth. He did not want for a thing to say. He explained why people have to die. Through the kindness of the Holy Ghost, he was able to explain our premortal existence, our probationary earth life, and what is in store for the faithful who have accepted God's gospel and endured to the end.

After he had talked for a few minutes, all of the people on the other side of the casket stood up and advanced toward him, until they were just across the casket from him. They took in every word with expressions of wonderment on their faces. They had never heard a message like this before. When he finished speaking, he glanced at his watch and noticed that his talk had lasted for twenty minutes.

Following the funeral services, Elder Paskett had the responsibility of dedicating the grave. The body was taken to a new graveyard located on a hill high above the town. There, the young man's body was buried, to await the time of the resurrection. To this day, Elder Paskett appreciates the great blessing that was bestowed upon him as he tried to fulfill his responsibilities as a priesthood holder.

Gift of Tongues

Missionaries Often Demonstrate the Gift of Tongues

" . . . In their more dramatic manifestations they [tongues and their interpretation] consist in speaking or interpreting, by the power of the Spirit, a tongue which is completely unknown to the speaker or interpreter. Sometimes it is the pure Adamic language which is involved. Frequently these gifts are manifest where the ordinary languages of the day are concerned in that the Lord's missionaries learn to speak and interpret foreign languages with ease, thus furthering the spread of the message of the restoration. When the elders of Israel, often in a matter of weeks, gain fluency in a foreign tongue, they have been blessed with the gift of tongues." (Bruce R. McConkie, *Mormon Doctrine*, 2d ed. [Salt Lake City: Bookcraft, 1966], p. 800.)

This Gift Often Counterfeited

"This is one of the most misunderstood gifts, and one which is a great cause of deception in the world. The Lord may use the dramatic method of speaking in tongues for the definite conveyance of an unusual message or for understanding a strange tongue, as on the day of Pentecost. Yet within the true Church it is a gift so often manifested by young missionaries who quickly grasp a foreign language that it is sometimes considered commonplace.

"Because this gift is often counterfeited and used to deceive, the Prophet Joseph Smith warned: 'Be not so curious about tongues, do not speak in tongues except there be an interpreter present; the ultimate design of tongues is to speak to foreigners.'" (*Doctrine and Covenants Student Manual* [Salt Lake City: The Church of Jesus Christ of Latter-day Saints, 1981], p. 101.)

The Purpose of This Gift Is to Help Others

"And again, it is given to some to speak with tongues;

"And to another is given the interpretation of tongues.

"And all these gifts come from God, for the benefit of the children of God." (D&C 46:24-26.)

22

Think of your brethren like unto yourselves,
and be familiar with all and free with your
substance, that they may be rich like
unto you.
—Jacob 2:17

I Gave Them
the Sleeping Bag

$\mathbf{A}$s Michael prepared to leave for his mission to Argentina, his Uncle Roger lent him a sleeping bag. His thought was that Michael could use the sleeping bag in areas where proper bedding was not available.

No thought was given to the sleeping bag after Michael left on his mission, until Roger received the following letter from his nephew:

"Dear Uncle Roger,

" . . . I'm so grateful for this chance that I've had to be a missionary and to see this world from a different point of view. One of the hardest things about my mission is having to see the poverty and suffering of these people. My heart just breaks and cries in anguish every time I have to see something like this. I would like to tell you about one of these experiences that I've had. This experience happened about a month ago.

"We had been teaching a very poor family for several months and had baptized a couple of members of their family.

One day we went by and found out that the father, who had been out of work for more than two years because of a serious illness, had been taken to the hospital. He spent about a month in the hospital. During this time, the mother had to go to the hospital every single day to take care of him. She missed many days from work and consequently lost her job. The debts began to pile up, and it wasn't long before they had to sell everything but the clothes on their backs and their little mud house.

"On one occasion when we visited the family, we found the mother just crying and in total desperation. She told us that it had been more than five days since she and her nine children had had anything to eat but some hot water. All of the children were running around in shorts and T-shirts, without shoes. They were just blue with the cold. I felt really guilty because I had just gotten up from a big lunch of mashed potatoes, steak, vegetables, and fresh baked rolls. I was also very comfortable, wearing my long johns, sweater, coat, gloves, and scarf. Roger, I don't know if you can see what I'm trying to tell you, but this was just more than I could handle. Both my companion and I went back to our apartment in tears. We knelt down and asked our Heavenly Father, 'Why?'

"He never answered us why, but he did guide us in our steps. After our prayer we both got up and, without saying anything, went through all of our belongings and selected things that we could do without and that they could use. We put these things in a box and then went to a little grocery store and bought them some things to eat. Roger, I don't want you to be mad at me, but in my overwhelming need to help this family, I gave them the sleeping bag that you lent me. Don't get me wrong, I shall never regret what I did, nor the feelings of love that we shared with this family. You should have seen the light in the eyes of the little children as we gave them each a pair of socks, a shirt, etc. It was funny to see the little tiny kids running around in my big socks; but, oh what joy I felt! When I gave the mother the sleeping bag and the box of food, she just lost all control and broke down into sobs and tears.

"It is such an awesome experience to be a missionary and to help spread our Savior's love. I know that He loves us. This knowledge has truly been a strength for me. I know that this family's knowledge that God loves them will be the only way for them to grow and to receive the strength they need to get through their problems.

"About a week after we took everything to this family, we found out that the father was dying of cancer and that he only had a few more weeks to live. They brought him home from the hospital so he could die at home.

"Sometimes life seems to so unfair. I know that we can never fully avoid tribulation, trial, separation, sorrow, distress, and difficulty. But through faith, understanding, and courage, we may truly prosper in the Spirit of the Lord.

"Roger, thanks for your gift and thanks for your love and strength in the Lord. Keep it up. I love you.

"Eternally yours,
Michael"

Helping the Needy

Walk Guiltless Before God

"And now, for the sake of these things which I have spoken unto you—that is, for the sake of retaining a remission of your sins from day to day, that ye may walk guiltless before God—I would that ye should impart of your substance to the poor, every man according to that which he hath, such as feeding the hungry, clothing the naked, visiting the sick and administering to their relief, both spiritually and temporally, according to their wants" (Mosiah 4:26).

Deal Mercifully with Your Substance

"I love that man better who swears a stream as long as my arm yet deals justice to his neighbors and mercifully deals his substance to the poor, than the long, smooth-faced hypocrite" (Joseph Smith, *Teachings of the Prophet Joseph Smith*, sel. Joseph Fielding Smith [Salt Lake City: Deseret Book Co., 1938], p. 303).

Service

Serve Your Fellow Beings

"And behold, I tell you these things that ye may learn wisdom; that ye may learn that when ye are in the service of your fellow beings ye are only in the service of your God" (Mosiah 2:17).

Ye Have Done It unto Me

"Tears came to my eyes when I read of a mere boy in one of our eastern cities who noticed a vagrant asleep on a sidewalk and who then went to his own bedroom, retrieved his own pillow, and placed it beneath the head of that one whom he knew not. Perhaps there came from the precious past the welcome words: 'Inasmuch as ye have done it unto one of the least of these my brethren, ye have done it unto me' (Matthew 25:40).

"I extol those who, with loving care and compassionate concern, feed the hungry, clothe the naked, and house the homeless. He who notes the sparrow's fall will not be unmindful of such service." (Thomas S. Monson, "A Doorway Called Love," *Ensign*, November 1987, p. 68.)

Through Another Person

"God does notice us, and he watches over us. But it is usually through another mortal that he meets our needs." (Spencer W. Kimball, *The Teachings of Spencer W. Kimball*, ed. Edward L. Kimball [Salt Lake City: Bookcraft, 1982], p. 252.)

Expand the Boundaries of Our Service

"We need to look around us, and if we cannot see poverty, illness, and despair in our own neighborhood or ward, then we have to look harder. And remember, we cannot be afraid to go beyond our own social and cultural circles. We have to rid ourselves of religious, racial, or social prejudices and expand the boundaries of our service. Service should never discriminate and is hardly ever easy." (Hans B. Ringger, "'Choose You This Day,'" *Ensign*, May 1990, p. 26.)

23

*But charity is the pure love of Christ,
and it endureth forever; and whoso is
found possessed of it at the last day, it
shall be well with him.*
—Moroni 7:47

Carlos

Most missionaries enjoy a lot of growth as they lose themselves in their missionary labors. Shane was one such missionary. He had been called to a mission in Brazil where the customs and living conditions of the people differed greatly from what he was used to. Shane shared the following experience with his mother in one of his letters. It describes the change that took place in him as his heart was filled with love for the people he had been called to serve.

"I've discovered a family here in Itu, that to me is very special. It is a family of six—a very poor family of six. I remember the first day here in Itu very vividly, because we ate lunch with this family. I remember the first thoughts I had of this family and the thoughts I had of their house—that is, if you want to call it a house. I was astonished and troubled at what I experienced that day.

"Even though I realized the living conditions would be very poor in some areas, this house was below anything I had imagined. I sat down on the bed—the only bed in the house—which happened to be in the kitchen and the living room and the bedroom, since this house only had one room. I honestly could not believe that these six people, and everything they owned, were crammed into a room the size of my bedroom.

"I recall the lunch they served me that day. My first thought was 'What are these people doing serving their food to me when they can hardly feed themselves?' They were so humble, and probably gave up eating in order to feed us missionaries. I guess I was not very humble or grateful, because I had a hard time eating the sticky rice and cold hard beans that seemed to attract every fly in the house. I just couldn't do it. What I wasted that day would probably have been greatly appreciated and enjoyed by the family.

"The whole time I was there I was looking forward to leaving that grungy, one-roomed house with the dirty little grubby kids, the dogs and cats running everywhere, and the cold sticky plate of rice and beans.

"Today I love those dirty grubby little kids with all of my heart. I've grown especially close to a little five-year-old boy by the name of Carlos. He has those big brown eyes that I love to look into. He is a very skinny little boy, but has a smile that can turn a strong man weak. I felt weak after seeing their house, clothes, and living conditions, and would have stayed weak except for Carlos. The love and hope I feel toward this family I gained through him.

"He looked me in the eyes and he winked when I winked. He made me smile when I smiled. He sat by my side and held my hand. That little five-year-old boy taught me a lesson that no man had ever taught me.

"I look forward to the days that I get to go see my little man Carlos. I love to shake his little hand and look into those big brown eyes. His eyes are always filled with light—a light that fills my soul with happiness. I love to pick up that little man and hold him in my arms. I love to sit by that little man in church and listen to him sing the hymns. He sings with dignity and with trust and with that perfect faith that only children can possess. My little man Carlos has that light—that light that brings out the pure love of Christ. I think of the scripture that says that we should humble ourselves as little children. I want to humble myself as a child—as my little man Carlos. Thank you Carlos. Thanks for the light that you have—the light you have shared with me."

Charity

As We Develop Charity We Become More like the Savior

"We must reach out beyond the walls of our own church. In humanitarian work, as in other areas of the gospel, we cannot become the salt of the earth if we stay in one lump in the cultural halls of our beautiful meetinghouses. We need not wait for a call or an assignment from a Church leader before we become involved. . . .

"When we get emotionally and spiritually involved in helping a person who is in pain, a compassion enters our heart. It hurts, but the process lifts some of the pain from another. We get from the experience a finite look into the Savior's pain as He performed the infinite Atonement. Through the power of the Holy Ghost, a sanctification takes place within our souls and we become more like our Savior. We gain a better understanding of what was meant when He said, 'Inasmuch as ye have done it unto one of the least of these my brethren, ye have done it unto me.'" (Glenn L. Pace, "A Thousand Times," *Ensign*, November 1990, p. 10.)

Service to Others Is Rarely Convenient

" . . . Opportunities to serve others are rarely convenient. Though some forms of service can be scheduled and performed upon assignment, much of the service we might give cannot be planned; it requires immediate, spontaneous, and—at times—prolonged attention. Elder William R. Bradford has observed that selfless service projects are not usually regulated, 'one-time special events.' Instead, they are ready responses to others' needs—'face-to-face, eye-to-eye, voice-to-ear, heart-to-heart, spirit-to-spirit, and hand-in-hand, people-to-people.' (*Ensign*,

November 1987, p. 75.)" ("The Visiting Teacher," *Ensign*, September 1990, p. 31.)

What Are the Qualities That Accompany Charity?

"And charity suffereth long, and is kind, and envieth not, and is not puffed up, seeketh not her own, is not easily provoked, thinketh no evil, and rejoiceth not in iniquity but rejoiceth in the truth, beareth all things, believeth all things, hopeth all things, endureth all things" (Moroni 7:45).

How Is Charity Obtained?

"But charity is the pure love of Christ, and it endureth forever; and whoso is found possessed of it at the last day, it shall be well with him.

"Wherefore, my beloved brethren, pray unto the Father with all the energy of heart, that ye may be filled with this love, which he hath bestowed upon all who are true followers of his Son, Jesus Christ; that ye may become the sons of God; that when he shall appear we shall be like him, for we shall see him as he is; that we may have this hope; that we may be purified even as he is pure. Amen." (Moroni 7:47-48.)

24

---

*But the Lord said unto Samuel, Look not on his
countenance, or on the height of his stature; because
I have refused him: for the Lord seeth not as man
seeth; for man looketh on the outward appearance, but
the Lord looketh on the heart.*

—1 Samuel 16:7

The Surprise
Call

Bishop Johnson had received word from his employer that
he was going to be transferred. He knew that this would
necessitate his release as a bishop. As he met with the stake
president and discussed his release, the stake president asked
him for some names of people in the ward whom they might
consider to replace him. Bishop Johnson quickly gave the stake
president the name of Brother Larsen, his first counselor.
Brother Larsen had been a counselor to two bishops, was well
liked by all the people in the ward, and was well prepared to
serve as a bishop. The stake president agreed that Brother
Larsen could make a fine bishop. He then asked Bishop Johnson for some more names. This took Bishop Johnson by surprise because he was so sure that Brother Larsen was the man
to be bishop. However, he gave the stake president the names
of everyone in the ward he thought might make a good
bishop.

Over the next few weeks, Bishop Johnson thought very

little about who would replace him, because he just knew Brother Larsen was the man for the job.

This all changed one night a few weeks before he was to be released. As he slept he had a dream. He saw himself in sacrament meeting. He dreamed that the stake president released him and then announced the name of the new bishop. The man who was named was not one of the names which he had given to the stake president. In fact, he had never even considered this man. The man was shy and quiet and not one who enjoyed leadership. The dream was so real and such a shock that he awoke suddenly and sat up in bed. Immediately the Spirit quietly spoke to his spirit and confirmed that this man indeed was to be the bishop. As he thought about why the Lord would give him such a dream, he was again instructed by the Spirit that it was his duty to share this experience with the ward members. He knew that he wasn't the only one whose list didn't include this man. None of the ward members would have picked this man to be bishop.

Bishop Johnson later found out that the night of his dream was the very night that the stake presidency made the decision for this man to be the bishop.

On the day of Bishop Johnson's release, to the surprise and wonder of the congregation, this man was presented and sustained as bishop. Brother Larsen was called to be his first counselor. As Bishop Johnson stood, he bore his testimony that this was the man the Lord wanted for bishop, and he shared with the congregation his experience with the dream.

This man went on to be one of the best bishops the ward had ever had. He came out of his shell and became a great leader. After he was released as bishop, he was called as a counselor in the stake presidency.

Bishop Johnson and the members of the ward learned a great lesson. The Lord sometimes is the only one who really knows our true potential. With his divine influence we can achieve many great things. He never asks us to do something without providing the help needed to succeed.

God's Wisdom and Power

God's Thoughts Are Higher Than Man's

"For my thoughts are not your thoughts, neither are your ways my ways, saith the Lord.

"For as the heavens are higher than the earth, so are my ways higher than your ways, and my thoughts than your thoughts." (Isaiah 55:8-9.)

All Things Are Possible with God

" . . . The things which are impossible with men are possible with God" (Luke 18:27).

All True Wisdom Comes from God

" . . . All true wisdom that mankind have they have received from God, whether they know it or not. There is no ingenious mind that has ever invented anything beneficial to the human family but what he obtained it from that One Source. . . . There is only one source from whence men obtain wisdom, and that is God, the fountain of all wisdom; and though men may claim to make their discoveries by their own wisdom, by meditation and reflection, they are indebted to our Father in heaven for all." (Brigham Young, in *Journal of Discourses* 13:148.)

God Does Great Things by Simple Means

"Now ye may suppose that this is foolishness in me; but behold I say unto you, that by small and simple things are great things brought to pass; and small means in many instances doth confound the wise" (Alma 37:6).

Calls to Serve

God Only Asks About Our Availability

" . . . God does not begin by asking us about our ability, but only about our availability, and if we then prove our dependability, he will increase our capability!" (Neal A. Maxwell, "It's Service, Not Status, That Counts," *Ensign*, July 1975, p. 7.)

We Can Achieve Miracles

" . . . When we qualify ourselves by our worthiness, when we strive with faith nothing wavering to fulfill the duties appointed to us, when we seek the inspiration of the Almighty in the performance of our responsibilities, we can achieve the miraculous" (Thomas S. Monson, "You Make a Difference," *Ensign*, May 1988, p. 43).

25

*But learn that he who doeth the works of
righteousness shall receive his reward,
even peace in this world, and eternal life
in the world to come.*
—D&C 59:23

Jesus Does!

All of us face difficult times in our lives. Sometimes the Lord intercedes and takes away our problems; other times he gives us the strength to cope with the obstacles we are facing. With his great knowledge and love, he knows what is best for us and acts accordingly. The one thing he does not do is leave us alone. If we will turn to him, we will find that he is always there. The following story bears testimony of this fact.

When Jeff was two years and nine months old, he was diagnosed as having a serious tumor. His parents were told that his chance of survival was only about fifteen percent. Elizabeth, his mother, knew the Lord could heal him; but she did not know whether or not he would. She realized that God sometimes says no.

The first week that Jeff had to have chemotherapy was a very difficult one for him and his parents. After the first treatment, Elizabeth sat down with Jeff and tried to explain to him what was happening. She told him that the treatment was hard, but that it was to help him feel better later and to make the tumor go away. She shared her love with him and assured him that Heavenly Father and Jesus loved him also. She promised Jeff that Heavenly Father and Jesus would help him through his sickness.

The next day Elizabeth realized that this message had somehow gotten through to Jeff, even though he was only two years old. He wore a shirt with the Incredible Hulk on it. When his nurse commented on his shirt and asked him if the Hulk helped him be brave, he answered, "No, Jesus does!"

That same morning his mother had overheard Jeff talking with his grandpa. Jeff had told his grandpa that he was a big boy. When his grandpa had asked him who told him that he was a big boy he had replied, "Jesus did!"

Elizabeth has often wished since that time that she had questioned Jeff about this; but the fact is, that Jeff showed exceptional bravery in the weeks to come. He faced going to the hospital each morning with some concern, but never with tears or tantrums, even at his young age. Elizabeth has always felt that it really was Jesus who helped him to be brave.

Jeff's health improved tremendously after receiving chemotherapy. Within six months the doctors felt that they had a good chance of removing the tumor. Jeff's parents were delighted at the news. Their joy soon turned to disappointment, however, as the surgery revealed that the tumor had spread to many of Jeff's vital organs.

Jeff showed courage and faith much beyond his years. At one time, shortly after his operation, Jeff and his mother were waiting to see the doctor at the Primary Children's Hospital. They could hear a child crying in the next room. Jeff was so concerned about the child that he had his mother say a prayer for him. Within a few seconds after finishing their prayer, the child stopped crying.

Jeff's health quickly went downhill. As Elizabeth left the hospital one night, her heart was heavy, for she knew that Jeff was going to die. As she walked across the parking lot, she saw a sparrow and remembered the words of Jesus when he said, "Are not two sparrows sold for a farthing? and one of them shall not fall on the ground without your Father [knowing it]. . . . Fear ye not therefore, ye are of more value than many sparrows." (Matthew 10:29, 31.) She felt the love of Heavenly Father and knew that he was watching over them and that he knew what they were going through.

The next night was Jeff's last night on this earth. Even though his mother was holding him, he would cry out, "Mom, are you there? Where are you, Mom?" She would assure him that she was there and, a few minutes later, he would cry out again. He suffered greatly that night, and Elizabeth and her husband prayed many times during the night that the Lord would take him before he suffered more.

The next morning his condition improved slightly, and he talked with his parents for a few minutes. Then he said to Elizabeth, "I'm all done, Mom. I'm all done." Within an hour or two, he was gone.

Heavenly Father blessed Jeff's family as they struggled to overcome their grief and heartache. One night when Elizabeth woke up with feelings of despair, the words of two Primary songs came to her. They brought her great comfort and helped her peacefully go back to sleep. The songs were "Did Jesus Really Live Again?" and "I Feel My Savior's Love in All the World Around Me."

One day, when the grief was severe, Elizabeth wondered why the other blessings in her life didn't help more to take away the pain and grief. She petitioned the Lord in prayer and asked him to help her to find comfort and to deal with her grief. The answer came that she had other children who needed her love very much and that she needed to work harder in both feeling this love and in showing it to her children. As she did this, Heavenly Father blessed her, and her heart received comfort.

Jeff's family feels that he was a very special child. They appreciate the great joy and love that he brought to their home. Every member of the family knows that Jeff loved them, and they love and miss him. With the help of the Lord, they have received the strength that they have needed to cope with their feelings, and they now enjoy the great blessings that life has to offer. They are happy and love one another and look forward to the time when Jeff will be part of their family again.

Inner Peace

No Problem Is Beyond the Help of Jesus

"Indeed there is no human condition—be it suffering, inca-pacity, inadequacy, mental deficiency, or sin—which [Jesus] cannot comprehend or for which His love will not reach out to the individual.

"He pleads today:

"'Come unto me, all ye that labour and are heavy laden, and I will give you rest.' (Matthew 11:28.)" (Ezra Taft Benson, "Jesus Christ," *Ensign*, June 1990, p. 6.)

Through His Suffering, Jesus Learned How to Succor His People

"And he shall go forth, suffering pains and afflictions and temptations of every kind; and this that the word might be ful-filled which saith he will take upon him the pains and the sick-nesses of his people.

" . . . and he will take upon him their infirmities, that his bowels may be filled with mercy, according to the flesh, that he may know according to the flesh how to succor his people according to their infirmities." (Alma 7:11-12.)

Peace Is Promised to the Righteous

"But learn that he who doeth the works of righteousness shall receive his reward, even peace in this world, and eternal life in the world to come.

"I, the Lord, have spoken it, and the Spirit beareth record." (D&C 59:23-24.)

Trials and Tribulation

Sorrow and Distress May Be Our Greatest Friends

"Being human, we would expel from our lives physical pain

and mental anguish and assure ourselves of continual ease and comfort, but if we were to close the doors upon sorrow and distress, we might be excluding our greatest friends and benefactors. Suffering can make saints of people as they learn patience, long-suffering, and self-mastery. The sufferings of our Savior were part of his education. 'Though he were a Son, yet learned he obedience by the things which he suffered; and being made perfect, he became the author of eternal salvation unto all them that obey him.' (Hebrews 5:8-9.)" (*Tragedy or Destiny?* [Salt Lake City: Deseret Book Co., 1977], p. 3.)

Peace Be unto Thy Soul

"My son, peace be unto thy soul; thine adversity and thine afflictions shall be but a small moment;

"And then, if thou endure it well, God shall exalt thee on high; thou shalt triumph over all thy foes." (D&C 121:7-8.)

These Things Shall Be for Thy Good

"If thou art called to pass through tribulation; if thou art in perils among false brethren; if thou art in perils among robbers; if thou art in perils by land or by sea; . . .

"And if thou shouldst be cast into the pit, or into the hands of murderers, and the sentence of death passed upon thee; if thou be cast into the deep; if the billowing surge conspire against thee; if fierce winds become thine enemy; if the heavens gather blackness, and all the elements combine to hedge up the way; and above all, if the very jaws of hell shall gape open the mouth wide after thee, know thou, my son, that all these things shall give thee experience, and shall be for thy good.

"The Son of Man hath descended below them all. Art thou greater than he?

" . . . therefore, fear not what man can do, for God shall be with you forever and ever." (D&C 122:5, 7-9.)

26

And no one can assist in this work except he shall be humble and full of love, having faith, hope, and charity, being temperate in all things, whatsoever shall be entrusted to his care.
—D&C 12:8

Miguel Had No Shoes

The vital attitudes of humility and gratitude were illustrated well by a young father, Miguel, who lived in the mountains of Guatemala. He was poor in terms of worldly possessions, but rich in testimony and faith. His shirt was ragged, his pants held together with more patches than original material, and he owned no shoes. He had received little formal education, could not read or write, and he made less than three hundred dollars a year.

Miguel served as a counselor in the small Church branch in his area. The branch met in a bamboo hut that was deteriorating rapidly. The roof sagged just a little bit more each week, stark evidence that the hut would not last much longer.

The missionaries in the area were teaching a young couple who were preparing for marriage, and they were overjoyed when the couple desired to be baptized. They planned to be married and baptized the same day.

On the selected day, the couple made the long bus trip to a neighboring city. The missionaries accompanied the couple and invited Miguel to travel with them. However, the marriage and baptism took longer than expected, so the return bus had already left. They could get a ride back to the main road, but that left them with a challenging walk of seventeen miles back to the area where they lived. Because of a serious gas shortage, they knew that there was little chance of a car driving by that would give them a ride.

The couple had some relatives in the city, so they could stay. But Miguel needed to get home so he could go to work the next morning. He and the missionaries set out to walk the seventeen miles. After walking for many hours, they came to the steep two-mile climb that would finally bring them home. One of the missionaries was murmuring to himself, asking God why they had to go through this physical torture. Then he glanced over at Miguel and saw a big smile on his face. This missionary could not think of anything to smile about after fifteen miles of walking, so he asked Miguel why he was so happy. Miguel's response taught him a great lesson, for he said, "I am so happy because we just witnessed two people become members of God's true Church." The missionary looked down at Miguel's bare feet, thought of the smile that had lasted for fifteen miles, and, through Miguel, came to realize how wonderful it was to introduce the gospel to others. His fatigue and anger were replaced with gratitude and humility for the opportunity they had received of teaching and baptizing a wonderful couple.

Just a few weeks later, the devotion of Miguel was illustrated even further. The bamboo chapel had deteriorated to the point that the last meeting was being held there. During the meeting, Miguel stood up and announced that he had been secretly building another chapel for the branch and that it was completed and ready to meet in. Miguel had to work twelve hours a day, six days a week, just to earn a meager living for his family; yet he had taken nearly every penny he made and all of his extra time during the previous six months to prepare a special meeting place. He still didn't have any shoes, but he had appreciated the gospel and the members so much that he had wanted to do something special for them and for the Lord. Because of his tremendous faith and dedication, the Lord had blessed him so that the needs of his family had been taken care of.

Humility and Gratitude

We Must Never Feel We Are Above Anyone

"A monk is said to have built a tower sixty feet high and three feet wide. On a certain day he would climb up to the top of the tower and pray, and the words of his prayers were generally about like this, 'Oh God, where art thou?' No answer. 'Oh God, where art thou?' No answer. Finally when he had exhausted someone's patience, there came a voice and it said, 'I am down among the people.' You have to be humble. Our wealth, our affluence, our liberties, all that we possess must never make us feel above anyone. We must always keep in mind a deep sincerity, a great humility, and a total dependence upon the Lord." (Spencer W. Kimball, "A Vision of Visiting Teaching," *Ensign*, June 1978, p. 28.)

God Has Chosen the Obscure and the Weak

" . . . Let an Elder hire the best halls in large cities to begin with, and go to lecturing, and it will take him a long time to raise a Branch of this Church. But let him begin among the poor of the earth—those who live in the cellars, and garrets, and back streets; 'for,' says the Almighty, 'I am going to take the weak things of the earth, and with them confound the wisdom of the wise.' You will see that trait in every step of 'Mormonism.' God has chosen the obscure and weak, to bring them up and exalt them." (Brigham Young, in *Journal of Discourses* 8:354.)

Humility Is Royalty Without a Crown

"Humility is royalty without a crown,
Greatness in plain clothes,
Erudition without decoration,
Wealth without display,
Power without scepter or force,
Position demanding no preferential rights,
Greatness sitting in the congregation,

Prayer in closets and not in corners of the street,
Fasting in secret without publication,
Stalwartness without a label,
Supplication upon its knees,
Divinity riding an ass."
(Spencer W. Kimball, "Humility," *Improvement Era*, August 1963, p. 704.)

Show Thanks by Proper Devotion

"In many countries, the homes are barren and the cupboards bare—no books, no radios, no pictures, no furniture, no fire—while we are housed adequately, clothed warmly, fed extravagantly. Did we show our thanks by the proper devotion on our knees last night and this morning and tomorrow morning?" (Spencer W. Kimball, *The Teachings of Spencer W. Kimball*, ed. Edward L. Kimball [Salt Lake City: Bookcraft, 1982], p. 120.)

27

. . . *Thou knowest the greatness
of God; and he shall consecrate
thine afflictions for thy gain.*
—*2 Nephi 2:2*

From Trials
to Blessings

Barbara was twenty-five years old when a virus in her heart left her unable to breathe without effort. She was constantly exhausted. When she would finally drift off to sleep, her heart would race and she would awaken, gasping for breath.

It was a frustrating time for Barbara. Prior to this time, she had been filled with energy and had used every bit of energy she had been blessed with. She had prided herself in being the best wife, mother, friend, and daughter that she could be. Her confinement was a frustrating, humiliating, and humbling experience. But she learned that some of the greatest lessons of life can be learned only through adversity.

Barbara found herself full of self-criticism. "A fine wife you turned out to be. And your children will never even know that they had a good mother; they are too young to remember." She belittled herself for not being able to do the wash, clean her house, or take care of her children, and for being such a burden to her husband.

Heavenly Father helped her to get rid of this depression in

several ways. First, because Barbara was so afraid of having a heart attack or of not being able to get another breath, she found herself in constant prayer. She soon found out that, while her physical body was in poor shape, her spirituality was soaring.

The second biggest help she received was through priesthood blessings. Dozens of times, she woke her husband during the night. Unable to catch her breath, she would ask him to give her comfort through a blessing. She also received hope that her heart would eventually heal. She asked her stake president to give her a blessing so that she could receive guidance about whether or not it would be possible for her to teach early morning seminary (a calling she'd been given prior to her illness). During that very special blessing, she was told that, if she was patient and wise in taking care of her physical needs, she would someday fully recover. She was also promised a special blessing of health for the time required to teach seminary every morning.

After this blessing, her hopes soared. She knew she wouldn't always be sick. This information (offered only through the blessing, not from a doctor or any other source) helped her to be patient.

The other promise of this blessing also came to pass: she was miraculously granted health during the early hours of her teaching mornings. She would get ready for seminary, drive fifteen miles to the church, set up the classroom, teach, and drive home. As she pulled in the driveway, she would feel the return of the effects of the illness. On Sundays she was so weak that she would have to lie on a lounge chair at church; but on each weekday morning, Barbara had the strength to teach.

The rest of each day was spent on the couch. Barbara watched sisters from her ward scrub her bathroom, vacuum her floors, and help in hundreds of ways with her children and her home.

She found that offering a listening ear can be as much help as baking bread or any other service. Even she, with her limited strength, could listen.

She taught her children to do things they never would have learned to do. Even though the oldest child was only five, each learned to do the laundry, clear the table, and fix simple meals.

She also gained compassion for others. She learned what it feels like to be ignored in a wheelchair, to think you are going to die, and to be unable to care for yourself or your family.

She also came to know the feeling of unconditional love. She knows she is loved for who she is and not for what she can do. Her family's love for her never changed, even when she could do nothing for them.

Over the course of the next three years, Barbara slowly regained her health and strength. But the lessons she learned through her illness will always stay with her and help her in helping others.

Afflictions

There Is Wisdom in His Giving Us Trials

"Is there not wisdom in his giving us trials that we might rise above them, responsibilities that we might achieve, work to harden our muscles, sorrows to try our souls? Are we not permitted temptations to test our strength, sickness that we might learn patience, death that we might be immortalized and glorified?" (Spencer W. Kimball, *The Teachings of Spencer W. Kimball*, ed. Edward L. Kimball [Salt Lake City: Bookcraft, 1982], p. 39.)

Suffering Makes Saints of People

"Being human, we would expel from our lives, sorrow, distress, physical pain, and mental anguish and assure ourselves of continual ease and comfort. But if we closed the doors upon such, we might be evicting our greatest friends and benefactors. Suffering can make saints of people as they learn patience, long-suffering, and self-mastery. The sufferings of our Savior were part of his education." (Spencer W. Kimball, *Teachings of Spencer W. Kimball*, p. 168.)

God Will Wipe Away All Tears

" . . . When George A. Smith was very ill, he was visited by his cousin, the Prophet Joseph Smith. The afflicted man reported: 'He told me I should never get discouraged, whatever difficulties might surround me. If I were sunk into the lowest pit of Nova Scotia and all the Rocky Mountains piled on top of me, I ought not to be discouraged, but hang on, exercise faith, and keep up good courage, and I should come out on the top of the heap.' (*George A. Smith Family*, comp. Zora Smith Jarvis [Provo: Brigham Young University Press, 1962], p. 54.)

"There are times when you simply have to righteously hang on and outlast the devil until his depressive spirit leaves you. As the Lord told the Prophet Joseph Smith: 'Thine adversity and thine afflictions, shall be but a small moment;

"'And then, if thou endure it well, God shall exalt thee on high' (D&C 121:7-8).

"To press on in noble endeavors, even while surrounded by a cloud of depression, will eventually bring you out on top into the sunshine. Even our master Jesus Christ, while facing that supreme test of being temporarily left alone by our Father during the crucifixion, continued performing his labors for the children of men, and then shortly thereafter he was glorified and received a fullness of joy. While you are going through your trial, you can recall your past victories and count the blessings that you do have with a sure hope of greater ones to follow if you are faithful. And you can have that certain knowledge that in due time God will wipe away all tears and that 'eye hath not seen, nor ear heard, neither have entered into the heart of man, the things which God hath prepared for them that love him' (1 Corinthians 2:9)." (Ezra Taft Benson, "Do Not Despair," *Ensign*, November 1974, p. 67.)

Endurance

God Is with Thee

"Be patient in afflictions, for thou shalt have many; but endure them, for, lo, I am with thee, even unto the end of thy days" (D&C 24:8).

The Measure of Greatness

" . . . Greatness is best measured by how well an individual responds to the happenings in life that appear to be totally unfair, unreasonable, and undeserved. Sometimes we are inclined to put up with a situation rather than endure. To endure is to bear up under, to stand firm against, to suffer without yielding, to continue to be, or to exhibit the state or power of lasting." (Marvin J. Ashton, "'If Thou Endure It Well,'" *Ensign*, November 1984, p. 22.)

Opposition Builds the Character of Man

"So it is with us today, we must also have the bitter in order to know the sweet. . . . This is normal. We all have our trials of life to *strengthen* us. Each thinks he has the hardest or most severe trials. It may be that they are the most difficult only because they are the hardest or most difficult for you. The diamond is enhanced and made more valuable with polishing. Steel is made harder and more valuable through tempering. So also opposition builds the character of man." (Eldred G. Smith, "Opposition in Order to Strengthen Us," *Ensign*, January 1974, p. 63.)

28

Now there must needs be a space betwixt the time
of death and the time of the resurrection.
And now I would inquire what becometh of the
souls of men from this time of death to the time
appointed for the resurrection?
—Alma 40:6-7

A Glimpse
Beyond the Veil

Mel received a call from a nursing home in Idaho where his father was a resident. They said he needed to come quickly because his father was in critical condition.

When he walked into his father's room, he was shocked to see his father hooked up to a life-support system. His father was one-hundred-three years old, and Mel felt uncomfortable with the situation—he felt that his father deserved to die with dignity. He and his sisters consulted with the doctors and made arrangements for the life-support to be removed.

They then went back to their father's room and visited with each other. Their father was not responsive, so they said their last good-byes and went to their father's home to await the phone call from the nursing home.

But when the call didn't come, they finally decided to go to bed.

The next morning, they went to the hospital to see what had happened. As they walked in his room, they were astonished to see their father sitting up in bed, eating a bowl of soup and a sandwich. They were shocked when he recognized them, and they were grateful to be able to have a good visit with him.

During a lull in the conversation, Mel's dad lay back in the bed and looked first at one side of the room and then at the other.

Mel's sister asked, "Dad, what are you looking at?"

He answered, "I'm looking at Mother, Louise, and the others."

Louise was Mel's little sister who had died at seven years of age. Mel asked, "Can you see them, Dad?"

"Yes," he replied, "and I can hear them talk."

Mel wanted to know more, so he asked, "Are they happy?"

"Oh, yes, they're happy. They're living in a state of forgiveness, repentance, and love." Then he added, "It is so bright and so beautiful."

Then Mel asked, "Would you like to be there, Dad?"

"Yes, I would love to be there. The light is so warm that you just want to go towards it."

"Then," Mel asked, "Why don't you go?"

His father replied, "Because I'm not the boss. When the boss wants me there, he'll call me."

Mel's father wasn't "called home" during that month or in the months that followed. His life was extended. But Mel and his sisters will be forever grateful for their father's sharing of his glimpse beyond the veil.

The Spirit World

The Departed Are Not Far from Us

" . . . The spirits of the just are exalted to a greater and more glorious work; hence they are blessed in their departure to the world of spirits. Enveloped in flaming fire, they are not far from us, and know and understand our thoughts, feelings, and motions, and are often pained therewith." (Joseph Smith, *Teachings of the Prophet Joseph Smith*, sel. Joseph Fielding Smith [Salt Lake City: Deseret Book Co., 1938], p. 326.)

The Spirit World Is Near

"As we approach this sacred hour when we will dedicate a new temple in a year or two or three, we expect that there are unseen visitors here, as one of the Brethren suggested. I expect that every one of the presidents of the Church, all twelve of us, have been dreaming glorious dreams about a temple in Tokyo. This world is not so far from the world of those who have passed on. We feel certain that they are permitted to visit the earth at times, and I think that Joseph Smith, Brigham Young, and all of the presidents, including Heber J. Grant, are surely not far from us this day." (Spencer W. Kimball, address given at Tokyo area conference, 10 August 1975, *The Teachings of Spencer W. Kimball*, ed. Edward L. Kimball [Salt Lake City, Bookcraft, 1982], p. 42.)

The Spirit World Is Close By

"There is always a great tendency for us to feel when we talk about people who have passed beyond, who have passed through the change called death, that they have gone some great distance away onto another planet or into another world. It is difficult for us to realize that the spirit world is close by, that it is all part of the operation here on this earth." (Ezra Taft Benson, *The Teachings of Ezra Taft Benson* [Salt Lake City: Bookcraft, 1988], pp. 30-31.)

United Again with Loved Ones

"I have a father, brothers, children, and friends who have gone to a world of spirits. They are only absent for a moment. They are in the spirit, and we shall soon meet again. The time will soon arrive when the trumpet shall sound. When we depart, we shall hail our mothers, fathers, friends, and all whom we love, who have fallen asleep in Jesus. There will be no fear of mobs, persecutions, or malicious lawsuits and arrests; but it will be an eternity of felicity." (Joseph Smith, *Teachings of the Prophet Joseph Smith*, pp. 359-60.)

The Spirit World Is Right Here

"When you lay down this tabernacle, where are you going? Into the spiritual world. Are you going into Abraham's bosom? No, not anywhere nigh there but into the spirit world. Where is the spirit world? It is right here." (Brigham Young, *Discourses of Brigham Young*, comp. John A. Widtsoe [Salt Lake City: Deseret Book Co., 1977], p. 376.)

Joyful Reunion in the Spirit World

"We have more friends behind the veil than on this side, and they will hail us more joyfully than you were ever welcomed by your parents and friends in this world; and you will rejoice more when you meet them than you ever rejoiced to see a friend in this life" (Brigham Young, *Discourses of Brigham Young*, pp. 379-80).

The Same Sociality Will Exist

"And that same sociality which exists among us here will exist among us there, only it will be coupled with eternal glory, which glory we do not now enjoy" (D&C 130:2).

29

*But when they in their trouble did
turn unto the Lord God of Israel,
and sought him, he was found of them.*
—2 Chronicles 15:4

The Message Had
Been Delivered

This is the story of the birth of a baby and the Lord's hand in the process. It was written in the baby's journal by her mother so that when the baby, Jenny Beth, grew up, she would know about the help of the Lord in her behalf. The following account contains selected parts from the journal which have been lightly edited for clarity. The journal entry was written directly to Jenny Beth.

"We were living in Grantsville, Utah. Our family had four children and one on the way. That one was you. We were all so happy. About this time Daddy applied to go to Germany for three years. He had always wanted to go overseas and had finally gotten the chance. Now, Jenny Beth, I guess you have to understand how I felt about going overseas, in order to understand just how special your birth was to me.

"First of all, I would have to leave Granny and Grandpa Jenkins. I loved them so much. When I was a little girl, I lived with them for several years. It was Granny who taught me how to make bread and bottle fruit. And Grandpa became my close friend and counselor. Their home became my favorite place on earth.

"They were growing old and I felt inside that, after we left for Germany, I would never see them in this life again. I would never again hug and kiss them, or smell the familiar odors of their home. I knew that I would see them in the next life, but that didn't stop the hurt I felt at the thought of leaving them behind. This was my first pain.

"Secondly, just a few months before, I had been sustained as the ward Relief Society president—and how I loved that calling! I loved the sisters that I worked with, and I loved those special spiritual things that happen to Relief Society presidents. Leaving this behind also was really more than my heart could bear.

"Shortly after arriving in Germany, I got an awful case of bronchitis. I would cough so hard that my tummy area, with you in it, would just ache. I've never hurt like that before or since. My chest felt like it was on fire.

"Then I had my first taste of socialized medicine. I went to the clinic to see a doctor and found that, instead of being Christy, I was, more or less, number 8342. I waited three hours, and then the doctor just gave me some cough syrup. I knew that I needed an antibiotic, but he wouldn't give me any. What was even worse was that he just didn't seem to care.

"When I arrived back at our quarters, I just cried and cried. The only thing that saved me was Sister Wright. She was my Relief Society president, and she just sort of 'loved me better.'

"The next few months passed slowly for me. I had several more awful experiences with the clinic. People there told me that I was a public health nuisance because of our five children, and said many other unkind things to me.

"About this time a wonderful thing happened. I found out that there was an honest-to-goodness, dyed-in-the-wool, Mormon obstetrician, working at the very hospital where you were to be born. His name was Dr. Duke. I felt that if I could just have him take care of me and deliver you, everything would be all right. If I could just have the priesthood there to take care of any problems that might arise, I could finally rest easy. This was something I hadn't done since that first visit to the clinic.

"Six weeks before you were due, I transferred to the clinic where Dr. Duke worked. When I asked if I could see him, they said that if I wanted a specific doctor, I would have to wait until everyone else was through. I told them that I would be happy to wait.

"Finally I got to see him. He was nice and pleasant as I had hoped he would be. I told him who I was and shared my sad story with him. I then asked him if he would be willing to special-deliver my baby. You see, in the army, doctors are assigned days of duty in advance, so whoever is on duty when you go into labor usually delivers your baby. I wanted to be certain he would be there for us.

"He asked me when you were due, and I told him the first part of June. That is when the miracle part of your birth began to unfold. He said that he would be glad to be my doctor, but that he would be out of the country during May and June. He said that, on May 19, he had to check in to receive new travel orders and that he would be in the clinic for one or two days at that time. He told me that, if I could manage to deliver you on May 19th, he would be glad to deliver you. I told him that I would take it up with my Heavenly Friend and see what could be done. We made an appointment for May 19th, just so he could check my progress.

"Well, Jenny, I took it up with the Lord. I poured out my heart to him and asked him to please, if it was all right with him, send you on May 19th. Each week when I visited the clinic, the doctors said that you wouldn't come until the middle of June. But I hoped that Heavenly Father had other plans.

"The 18th of May was a Sunday. We were at sacrament meeting when Heavenly Father began to weave his miracle. My labor pains began and, as the rest of the day progressed, so did my labor. Things slowed down that night, so we slept, and waited for my doctor's appointment the next morning.

"Monday, May 19th, 1975, was a day of testimony that miracles do happen. My labor began again, and we headed for the clinic. Dr. Duke was there, as scheduled, and said to me, "Well, what have you got to say for yourself?" I just grinned and said, "I told you I would take it up with my friend." When he examined me, he found that you, dear Jenny, were on your way from one home to another.

"That night you were born, and I was so happy that I cried and cried. You brought a lot of sunshine back into my life, and I was happier than I had been for months.

"So you see, your coming was really a special one. I know for sure that Father heard and answered my prayer in faraway Germany.

"He also did something else that I want you to know about. While I was still pregnant with you, I just wanted you to know something. So one night, when I was saying my prayer, I asked Father if he would tell this sweet, new baby that I was going to have, how much I already loved her, how I would work hard to teach her the gospel and help her return back to him again. I just wanted you to know, Jenny, even before you were born, how dear you were to me, and how I would be your friend as well as your mother. When I finished my prayer, I was told by the Holy Ghost that you knew—that the message had been delivered."

God Loves Us

As Children of God, We Are Precious to Him

"Man is greater and grander, more precious according to the arithmetic of God, than all of the planets and suns of space. For man were they created. They are the handiwork of God. . . . Man is his son." (J. Reuben Clark, Jr., from LDS film *This Is My Glory.*)

Heavenly Hosts Are Pulling for Us

"God loves us. He's watching us, he wants us to succeed, and we'll know someday that he has not left one thing undone for the eternal welfare of each of us. If we only knew it, there are heavenly hosts pulling for us—friends in heaven that we can't remember now, who yearn for our victory. This is our day to show what we can do." (Ezra Taft Benson, from "Insights," *Ensign*, July 1975, p. 63.)

God Is Involved in Our Lives

"And he gathereth his children from the four quarters of the earth; and he numbereth his sheep, and they know him; and there shall be one fold and one shepherd; and he shall feed his sheep, and in him they shall find pasture" (1 Nephi 22:25).

God Desires to Dwell with Us

"Jesus answered and said unto him, If a man love me, he will keep my words: and my Father will love him, and we will come unto him, and make our abode with him" (John 14:23).

Prayer

What Should We Include in Our Prayers?

"For what should we pray? We should pray about our work, against the power of our enemies and the devil, for our welfare and the welfare of those around us. We should counsel with the Lord regarding all our decisions and activities. We should be grateful enough to give thanks for all we have. We should confess his hand in all things." (Ezra Taft Benson, "Pray Always," *Ensign*, February 1990, p. 4.)

God Will Support Us in Time of Need

"But when they in their trouble did turn unto the Lord God of Israel, and sought him, he was found of them" (2 Chronicles 15:4).

If We Diligently Seek God, We Will Find Him

"Draw near unto me and I will draw near unto you; seek me diligently and ye shall find me; ask, and ye shall receive; knock, and it shall be opened unto you.

"Whatsoever ye ask the Father in my name it shall be given unto you, that is expedient for you." (D&C 88: 63-64.)